The Distinctive

A Report to the Board of Ministry, The Diocese of Salisbury

January 2003

Published by Sarum College Press on behalf of the Diocese of Salisbury.

ISBN 0 9534836 1 4

Sarum College Press
19 The Close, Salisbury
Wiltshire SP1 2EE
01722 326899
bookshop@sarum.ac.uk
www.sarumcollegebookshop.co.uk

The Distinctive Diaconate

A Report to the Board of Ministry,
The Diocese of Salisbury

January 2003

The Working Party's brief:
To clarify our theological and practical understanding of the diaconate in order to focus ministerial policy for the next ten years.

Members of the Working Party:
The Revd Rosalind Brown (Chair)
Vice Principal, Ordained Local Ministry Scheme and Academic Staff Member of The Southern Theological Education and Training Scheme (STETS).

Canon Chrysogon Bamber
Sarum Reader and Vice Warden of Readers, Diocese of Salisbury.

The Revd Canon Jeremy Davies
Precentor, Salisbury Cathedral

The Revd Margaret Jackson
Convenor, Southern Regional Theological Network (until April 2002) and Associate Staff member STETS. Assistant Priest at The Bourne with Tilford, Farnham, Guildford Diocese and Ministerial Consultant to Gloucester Diocese.

The Revd Roy Overthrow
Deacon. Bishop's Deacon (until April 2002), Assistant Curate, Marlborough Team (from May 2002)

The Revd Andrew Sinclair
Vicar, Verwood

'... in order to focus ministerial policy for the next ten years.'

Foreword by the Bishop of Salisbury

The origins of this report lie in two convictions. First, that a coherent theology of ministry should reflect what the church is called to reveal about Christ, and not merely about either the historical practice of the church or a limitedly functional understanding of what Christian ministers do. And second, that the ministry of the deacon is foundational for all Christian ministry, and should be reinvigorated in the life of the church as a whole and in the diocese in particular.

What are the implications of this for the way in which we grow and select ministers? What are the criteria by which we should assess a distinctively diaconal call to ministry? What kind of distinctive formation should deacons receive before any thought is given as to whether they might also be candidates for priestly ministry? These were some of the initial questions in our minds when the report was commissioned.

At the heart of this report lies a theology of ministry derived from reflection on the work of Christ, and the way in which his coming among us and his death and resurrection have shaped the church since. This is the theology of ministry that we have worked with over these recent years when we have explored a renewed pattern of vocation, which has led to our Ordained Local Ministry (OLM) scheme. It has also had some influence on the early drafts of the revised Ordinal.

A theology of ministry begins with Christ handing over to his church the responsibility of continuing his ministry. Every baptized person who has tumbled to it that this is what they are is called to use their gifts to minister in his name. But while each of us has a ministry, not all of us are called to be ministers. Ministers are ordained to hold before the church a specific focus of Christ's ministry – his sharing our life, his redemptive transformation of it and his handing over to us the responsibility of continuing this pattern of engagement and transformation.

Within the ministry of all the baptized, this threefold pattern of God's activity in response to our human story is expressed in the historic threefold ministry of the Church. To the broken, self-absorbed world of human striving God in

Christ comes among us, raises us up and equips us to live his life. This saving activity of Incarnation, Redemption and Sanctification is given visible focus in the life of the Church by the three historic orders of ministry. It is these Orders that give a Christ-like shape to the Church and remind the whole church, not just the ordained, that we are his body and that we minister in his name and by his strength alone.

The ministry of a Deacon

The Incarnation is the foundation of God's redeeming activity. It comes first. 'That which God did not assume, he did not redeem' says Gregory Nazianzus, making it clear that for God to change people, he needed first to engage with us and share human life. In the same way, the ministry of the deacon is the foundation of all ordained ministry. You are a deacon first and, even if later you become a priest or a bishop, you never cease to be a deacon. The Incarnation is about God coming among us to share our life, and setting aside the trappings of pomp and power. (Philippians 2.5-11). The Deacon focuses this sense of God sharing our life and engaging with us directly by making God's incarnation, his becoming rooted in human life, central in the Church. Priests and bishops who forget that they are deacons too often try and use their position to get their own way, forgetting that Jesus taught us differently – that authority and kingship are rooted in service, not in the capricious use of power. (It shall not be so among you... Matthew 20.26). This is the heart of what ministry means, though Government Ministries and even Prime Ministers do not always seem to act as if they know this! Perhaps this is because we have lost the sense of the ordained as signposts to the whole of the *laos* or people of God of whom they are a part. So often we have colluded with a theology of ministry that says the ordained are there to minister *instead* of the whole people rather than saying that the ordained are to be *a focus*, a constant reminder, for what every Christian is called to be. This is why the ordained carry the church's authority to minister in a representative way.

In coming among us to share our life and engage with us face to face, God in Christ draws his disciples into a ministry of love and service by washing his disciples' feet, commanding them to go and do likewise. In John 13, Jesus teaches by example. When that gospel is read at the Ordination of Deacons, and even more when the Bishop washes his newly-ordained deacons' feet, we are reminded of just how fundamental this ministry is, and how often we are tempted to try and bring a change to people without that necessary engagement first. The Deacon's ministry is about this kind of engagement with the particularities of human life. That is why a deacon is appointed to serve in a particular place, to take root in a community, just as the Christ was born in a particular place - Bethlehem – at a particular time - 2000 years ago.

It is also why in worship it has traditionally been the deacon who has brought the book of the Gospels into the assembly and been charged with reading the Gospel among the people, with gathering up the particularities which give substance to the prayers of intercession, with preparing the table and distributing the Holy Communion, with translating this sense of renewed commitment into practical tasks of being the church in the coming week, and with sending out the assembled church to do them. This sense of being God's agent, the go-between who engages with the task, means that deacons are active in the community, which is why they wear their stoles tied round their albs, so that they are ready for action.

The ministry of the priest

If the focus of a deacon's ministry is the Incarnation, the focus of a priest's is the Redemption. If a deacon shows to the Church how God in Christ shares our life, the priest reveals how God in Christ changes it. That is why the priest is the minister who presides over the sacraments, those rites in the church where we celebrate the reality of the change that God in Christ brings about. Whether we are talking of baptism or the eucharist, individual change or corporate renewal, the same is true. The priest's task is to reconcile, to draw people and communities together; to bless people in God's name; to preach and teach so that people's lives are changed; and to intercede like that great High Priest 'who ever lives to make intercession for us'. (Hebrews 7.25)

At the heart of the priest's life is the one, perfect self-offering of Christ to the Father. This sacrificial action has what St Paul describes as 'the upward call of God in Christ Jesus' (Philippians 3.14) as its theme, and transformation as its key. The power to change is not one of manipulation to get what we want; it is the surrender of our wills to God's, that his kingdom come, his will be done. This is the mystery of the cross, which looks like a failure to the unbeliever, but turns out to be the power of God, perfected in our human weakness. The resurrection turns the cross upside down; the tree of death becomes the tree of life; where life was lost, there life has been restored. This reversal, this turning of the world's expectations upside down, is the heart of the mystery of the eucharist, where the priest takes the one bread he or she has just consecrated to be the body of Christ, and breaks it into pieces, that we, the broken members of Christ's body all may receive a fragment of that broken bread and so be restored to life and union with God.

The priestly life, then, has as its focus a sense of being drawn into the sacrificial self-offering of Christ to the Father; it is a life of constant tension and continuous change, and the challenge is to hold this pattern of continuing change before the whole church as a never-ending challenge to our being satisfied with where we've got to.

The ministry of a bishop

The bishop is still both priest and deacon. The bishop is rooted in the particularity of the diocese, which is why a bishop must live there among the people. The bishop is there to engage with them, to listen to them and to serve them; this is made visible when the bishop washes the feet of the newly ordained deacons at an ordination. Still a priest, the bishop continues the ministry of reconciliation, drawing people by word and example into the body of Christ, the wounded healer, that we may be drawn into his perfect self-offering to the Father.

But the bishop's most distinctive ministry is to hand on the apostolic witness to the risen Christ: 'I delivered to you what I also received, that Christ Jesus was raised ...' (I Corinthians 15.3). But you can only hand on a tradition if there is a continuing community into which people are being woven all the time. So the focus of the bishop's ministry is building the community of faith, so that the tradition may be handed on. This is most visible when baptising and confirming new Christians and ordaining deacons and priests.

Confirmations and Ordinations also mark the moment where the church in all its diversity can be recognised to be essentially one with the Spirit-filled tradition of the early apostles. The day of Pentecost (Acts 2) reverses the consequences of the Tower of Babel (Genesis 11): the same phenomenon – a rich diversity of tongues – is seen not as a sign of chaos or fragmentation, but – to a church looking outwards – as a sign of engagement with all God's people everywhere. This leadership in turning outwards, in mission, is another responsibility of the bishop. A bishop's crook or pastoral staff has two ends: a hook to draw people together in unity, and a sharp end to prod them into action.

The bishop does not do this because he or she possesses some power of his own. The bishop exercises his or her ministry to order and shape the church in order to make visible the commission given by Christ to his apostles to draw everyone into one fold, and to baptise all nations. The bishop is the sign of the continuing activity of the Spirit in the church to draw people into unity and to energise them for mission.

The diaconate

Within this Christologically rooted theology of ministry in the church, the report that follows concentrates on the diaconate. It builds on the work of the Church of England's working party *'For such a time as this'*, published in 2001, and on the experience of the diaconate in the diocese of Portsmouth and elsewhere in the Church of England. Its principal author is Rosalind Brown, the Vice-Principal of the Salisbury OLM Scheme and staff member of the Southern Theological Education and Training Scheme, based in Sarum College. Her experience of the diaconate in ECUSA has been invaluable, in addition to her theological skills and her gift for lucid and persuasive writing. I am grateful to her and to all who have helped her in this enterprise, which we hope will be of interest to the whole church, and not just to the diocese of Salisbury.

+ David Sarum
27th February 2003

Introduction

In 2001 the Board of Ministry of the Diocese of Salisbury established a Working Party to explore the diaconate as a distinctive ministry, rather than just as a transitional ministry prior to ordination to the priesthood. In this report, which was initially discussed by the Board of Ministry in October 2002, and approved in January 2003, the Diocese affirms the distinctive ministry of the deacon in the total ministry of the church.

The report is not written in a vacuum. The theological and ecclesiological context for discussions on the diaconate has been shaped by earlier papers in the Diocese, specifically the OLM submission, Bishop David's papers 'Celebrating Ordination' and 'The Diaconate', and the Revd. Dr Ian Paul's paper, 'Reflections on the Diocesan Theology of Ministry'. We have, in addition, drawn on writing from other sources outside the diocese including the report to the General Synod of the Church of England, 'For such a time as this'.[1] We are grateful for comments on the first draft of this report from the Revd. Dr Ian Paul and the Revd. Sue Woan, and to the Revd. Dr. Roly Riem who has been an ongoing dialogue partner in the latter stages of the report's production.

We take as a given the threefold order of bishops, priests and deacons set alongside the ministry of the laity which is expressed both through authorised ministries of Reader, Lay Pastoral Assistant, Church Army Officer, Deaconess, and in many other ways as people offer their gifts in the parishes. In taking this threefold order as given, we try to make sense of it in the context of the Church of England in the twenty first century. This threefold ordering of ordained ministry evolved from the primitive and diverse patterning of ministry in the apostolic church. It is not of the essence of the church, but it is an Anglican belief (affirmed in the Lambeth Quadrilateral) that it contributes to the well-being of the Church and the continuity of Anglican identity. The threefold order has not always been seen as a vital aspect of the Church's life, still less has it been used as an instrument of mission. We believe, however, that this basic ministerial structure — albeit one that has embraced many forms and functions over time — is a gift from God to the church. In our own time it can serve to animate other ministries and to deepen the communion and apostolicity of God's people.[2]

With the benefit of hindsight, we recognise that one of the reasons that 'For such a time as this' stumbled at General Synod was the perceived lack of clarity between the distinctive ministries of deacons and Readers. Through the discussions on this report, we are also aware of a lack of understanding of the threefold order which leads to the mistaken assumption in some quarters that the diaconate is 'yet another ordained ministerial layer'[3] that both duplicates the ministry of priests and disempowers lay people. Our hope and expectation is that recognition of the distinctive ministry of deacons will further the collaborative ministry of all members of the church.

In the first section of the report, we summarise some of the theological and ecclesiological thinking from other sources that has influenced our discussions. This is followed in section 2 by some of our own thinking, either in response to the work of others or as a development of issues that have arisen as part of our work. Later sections of the report summarise the current situation in various churches, the practical issues that need to be considered and recommendations for action in this diocese.

1. The Theological Context of Diaconal Ministry: Summaries of some existing work

1.1 Diocese of Salisbury

The theology of ministry in this diocese as described in the diocesan reports[4] is governed by the fundamental Christian principles of incarnation and redemption. All baptised Christians share in the ministry of the church, continuing Christ's ministry. There is a commitment to collaborative ministry and to the ministry of all the baptised. Whilst all are called to minister, not all are called to be ministers. This is leading to a renewed understanding of the function and purpose of the ordained minister within the ministry of the whole church, since ordination makes visible in a particular person a distinctive call to the universal ministry of the church. Ordination places a person within that catholic order, it is not primarily concerned with the way in which that ministry will be exercised in a local context.

In recent years the commitment to Ordained Local Ministry represents an understanding of the minister in a local place as a 'representative person' rooted in a village or community who provides continuity and local knowledge, complementing the ministry of other clergy and very often 'owned' by the community as their person. The emergence of OLMs highlights the importance of a person being ordained in the first instance to the diaconate, as a public role develops out of an embryonic ministry which the person has already been fulfilling for the community. This raises the question, central to our work, of whether this vocation to be deacon in a local community might be to a more permanent ministry as deacon rather than a transitional stage on the way to ordination as a priest. Such a diaconal vocation could be indicated where the incarnational rootedness is a stronger pull inwards to the community than any outward pull to the challenge of transformation, which may be expressed in a priestly vocation.[5]

Within the total ministry of the church, each order highlights a particular aspect of Christ's work and holds this before the church. The diaconate focuses God's engagement with us, his sharing our nature in Christ's incarnation, coming among us in the form of a servant and being rooted in the particularity of time and place. This rootedness opens the door to a ministry of attention, service and the brokering that goes with the concept of Christ as 'agent'. Without this rootedness there is no possibility of redemptive change being effective. Priests need to remember that they are deacons too and to spend time in diaconal engagement in order to be rooted in reality: there are parallels with our Lord spending 30 years in preparation for 3 years of active ministry.

Another central facet of diaconal ministry is the exemplification of the interdependence of worship and service in the church's life. Deacons share in the liturgical leadership of the people of God and exercise a ministry of love within the community. From early times there has been a particular link between the bishop and the deacons whose ministry should enable the bishop to perform his social and caring ministry. But it is not only the bishop whose ministry is affected by the deacons, the ministry of lay people should be developed rather than inhibited by the ordination of deacons who model Christian ministry to others.[6]

1.2 'For such a time as this'

The most recent report on the diaconate in the Church of England, 'For such a time as this', was published in 2001. It summarises ecumenical developments in theology and practice. It recognises the breakthrough that occurred in 1982 with the Lima Document, 'Baptism, Eucharist and Ministry' (BEM)[7] and refers to the paragraph from BEM which speaks of deacons representing to the church its calling as servant in the world, and their exemplification of the interdependence of worship and service. It also recognises that some administrative work may fall, appropriately, to deacons. It describes the significant shift that occurred with BEM as the move from a structural and hierarchical approach to ordained ministry towards a more integrated ecclesiological approach that grounds ordained ministry in the nature and mission of the church. This is reflected in the theology of ministry in this diocese.

'For such a time' as this describes the very significant dialogues between the Anglican and Lutheran churches which recognise that apostolicity is intrinsic to the church and must be predicated of particular ministries. The Hanover Report (1996) insists on the deacon being rooted in the ordered life of the church and its liturgy and says that this should have a multiplying effect, leading and resourcing others in their own ministries. 'For such a time as this' summarises the effect of the more consistently ecclesiological approach to ordained ministry since BEM as being to encourage us to see ministry as dependent on the empowering of the Holy Spirit, with each order of ministry having a distinctive commission though without pretending that the set of tasks assigned to any particular order is completely exclusive.[8]

When 'For such a time as this' turns to the question of renewal in the theology of ministry, both lay and ordained (chapter 5) it stresses that the idea of representative ministry is fundamentally relational. Ministry is representative of both Christ and the Church – of Christ in and through his Body. This theme of representativeness brings ministry into close relationship with community, and it also requires authorisation from those one represents. It recognises that all Christians, through faith and baptism, represent Christ to their neighbour, the whole church is sent by Christ into the world and is therefore apostolic, but that representativeness is differentiated in various ministries. In relation to the diaconate that representativeness needs to be clarified. Ministry, being publicly acknowledged and publicly accountable, is something more than Christian discipleship which is not necessarily public, representative or formally accountable.

Ordained ministers are given authority to speak and act in a public, representative way that goes beyond what lay people are authorised to do, and they are set apart for this ministry for life. The primary ministry is that of Christ himself and they carry out their ministry in Christ's name, not their own, in ways that are laid down in the law of the church. BEM recognises the ecumenical agreement that their ministry is constitutive for the life and witness of the church. The Incarnation, with its self-emptying and self-offering for the sake of those God so loved is the model of all Christian ministry.

'For such a time as this' places considerable weight on the 1990 work of the Australian New Testament scholar, John Collins[9]. Collins questions the received understanding of *diakonia* as being primarily service, particularly humble service. Whilst there is biblical foundation for this, for example in Philippians 2, Collins' work suggests wider meanings. In addition to the recognised derivation from the concept of serving or waiting on table, Collins suggested further valid meanings of *diakonos* as spokesperson, envoy, courier, go-between entrusted with important tidings, as ambassador, mediator, person given a commission to carry out a task and act on behalf of a person in authority, and as attendant upon a person within a household on whose behalf one performs various tasks that are not limited to waiting at table. These can be summarised under the three categories of deacon as bearer of a message, deacon as agent and deacon as attendant. Collins draws out the crucial common elements in classical Greek usage of responsible agency on behalf of a person in authority and commitment to fulfil a vital task. He discounts any connotations of inferiority or menial service. This fundamental meaning derived from secular society is carried into New Testament usage, in particular Paul understands himself as a *diakonos* with the Lord's commission. In the second century Ignatius of Antioch wrote to the Trallians that deacons must be shown respect since they represent Jesus Christ, just as the bishop has the role of the Father and the presbyters are like God's council. The New Testament word for servant or slave is not *diakonos* but (normally) *doulos*.

After examining three dimensions of the work of Christ in the world through the church, *martyria* (witness), *leitourgia* (worship) and *diakonia* (service), 'For such a time as this' explores new insights into the work of the deacon. The deacon is invested with authority by Christ, through the Church in the person of the bishop. The deacon is not set apart for menial service nor is expected to exhibit more humility than others or to bear more than his or her fair share of suffering for Christ's sake. Instead, the deacon is a person on mission, a messenger or ambassador, making connections, building bridges, faithfully delivering his or her mandate. The deacon is the visible sign of what the Church is called to be, representing to the Church and to the world its authoritative calling as the servant of God and God's people. The deacon, like all the ordained, is to promote, release and clarify the nature of the Church. The deacon is an ecclesial sign and in ordination receives an ecclesial identity that relates to the Kingdom of God and to the place and role of the Church in God's coming kingly reign. Christ is the embodiment of the Kingdom and the archetypal baptised one, Deacon, Priest and Bishop.

The report goes on to say that whilst each ordained ministry is distinctive they also overlap with each other and with the ministry of lay people. This is seen as inevitable because the work entrusted to the Church is an integrated whole not a random assortment of discrete functions. The doctrine of the Trinity, with its differentiation of persons in unity of being, is the paradigm. The diaconate (like the presbyterate and episcopate) not only reflects what is true of all Christians but is the *sine qua non* of all ordained ministry, the template on which it is fashioned.[10]

1.3 'The Ministry of the Deacon'

Two volumes entitled 'The Ministry of the Deacon'[11] bring together many papers from the Anglo-Nordic Diaconal Research Project (ANDREP). This research project grew out of conversations organised by the Nordic Ecumenical Council in 1995 and has the support of the Church of England's Council for Christian Unity. These papers contain much very useful information about the ministry of the deacon in various countries and churches. In terms of theology and ecclesiology, it is clear that many different understandings undergird the ministry of the deacon and any translation of the practice of one country to another must take account of the respective ecclesiological underpinnings. In the Lutheran Church, the ordained ministry is seen to be by nature one, not threefold, and has been understood in the narrow sense of a preaching office. This means that in many Lutheran churches the diaconate is not understood as an ordained order, but there are differences between Lutheran churches on this. Dialogues between Lutherans and Anglicans have highlighted some of the ecumenical consequences that flow from the definition of ordained ministry as a preaching office, and Lutherans are beginning to ask if 'the Word' can be understood in a wider context so that diaconal ministry is a ministry of the Word.

In terms of specific differences, some churches understand the diaconate to be an ordained order, others a lay order; some deacons have a significant liturgical role others have none; some recognise as deacons those people whose professional training equips them for the care of people, others seek a clear diaconal vocation that may or may not be expressed primarily in the care of others. In some Lutheran churches deacons work primarily through the church, in others they work much more as arms of the civic authorities.

The legacy of the nineteenth century deaconess movement based at Kaiserswerth (see section 1.4 for further information) is fundamental to many of these differences, particularly the distinction between diaconal ministry that springs from the church calling a person to the office of a deacon and diaconal ministry that springs from a person having professional training and offering themselves to the church (for ordained or lay diaconal ministry) on the basis of that professional skill. At heart the question is 'does the vocation or the skill come first, and who initiates the identification of the vocation?' And following from this is the question, raised by ANDREP, of whether the deacon's identity forms the diaconal spirituality or the deacon's personal spirituality determine the diaconal identity?

1.4 Lay ministries in the Church of England: Readers and Deaconesses

Another significant consideration is the theology and ecclesiology that underlies lay ministries in the Church of England. Very often this is tacitly rather than explicitly expressed, and some of the current confusion about the relationship of different ministries to each other derives from this lack of clarity. We have in mind, in particular, the heritage we receive of the ministry of deaconesses in the Church of England, and the ministry of Readers. In both cases the roots lie in the nineteenth century and the desire to provide opportunities for suitably trained lay women and men to serve the church. The ministry of Readers also has roots in earlier minor orders of lector and sub deacon, whilst the deaconesses express the long-standing ministry of care for the needy, some of which was provided by monastic orders in earlier centuries. It appears that the theology and ecclesiology of these two ministries were not thought through at the time they were introduced into the Church of England and although some work has been done since, particularly in the case of Readers, this has followed rather than led the emergence of these ministries and tends to describe what now exists.

The recent book on Reader ministry, 'Bridging the Gap'[12], is almost entirely focused on some of the practicalities of Reader ministry, its theological and ecclesiological foundations are simply assumed whilst the gap referred to in the title is not defined or explored in any depth. Carolyn Headley, in her

Grove book on Reader ministry[13], notes that there are a number of reports and documents over recent years that provide guidance for good practice, draw attention to the issues that Readers face and encourage Reader ministry. However, she does not refer to work on the theology of Reader ministry and her opening paragraphs on the nature of Reader ministry express the anxiety that some feel about where Readers 'fit into' the ministry of the church. This mirrors the request by one of the Readers speaking in the General Synod on the diaconate who asked that the ordained 'help us to sort out our ministry.'[14]

Although Headley does not address theological and ecclesiological issues directly, she does identify the distinctiveness of the calling of a Reader as lying not in function but in their identity as theologically trained lay people whose ministry is recognised not only locally but in the wider church. Readers can be the focus of lay ministry which needs to be part of the daily life of the church. Their liturgical role speaks of the value of the laity and recognises the distinctive contribution and worth of their ministry which is a complementary ministry bringing the *laos* into the focal point of the church's life, the worship. It is not only a focus but a role model or flagship. Greater participation of the laity in the liturgy gives the visible message that it is the whole church family that is worshipping together, speaks of God's desire to work in and through each one of us, and of the presence of the Holy Spirit in all believers. Reader ministry ensures that those with known gifts and abilities are not denied their ministry, and the Reader's calling is not only to be a focus for all lay ministry but also to positively enable, nurture and encourage the calling of all laity to use their God-given gifts. The fact that Readers are admitted to a canonical office and receive a licence to minister gives them authority which needs to arise in the first place from that given by God, evidenced by gifts which are recognised by the congregation and incumbent. She notes that if Readers define themselves by the function of their ministry they can feel threatened by the diverse authorisation of other lay ministries that exist. However, if they see Readership as the principal canonically recognised lay ministry then it is the office to which widely gifted men and women are licensed, leaving those with more distinct but limited spheres of ministry to be authorised by more specific episcopal permission.

The situation with deaconesses is described by Christine Hall in part of her contribution to the dialogue with the Nordic churches.[15] It illustrates the lack of theological forethought when, in the nineteenth century, the Church of England created a group of women ministers which it called deaconesses. They were not made deaconesses with the same rite used for (male) transitional deacons and although some deaconesses claimed they had a direct relationship with the deacons of the early church and the contemporary order of deacons, this was never accepted officially. Instead, the ministry of deaconesses was shaped by the Kaiserwerth Diaconal Institution in Germany. There, women lived in a Mother House and received either nursing or teacher training, along with religious instruction. Once trained, most continued to work in institutions although a few worked in parishes. The first deaconess in England was admitted in 1862 and soon they were widely recognised. They had to remain unmarried and normally worked from a parish rather than an institutional base, although they lived in together in deaconess households. (The requirement of celibacy, later abandoned, appears to reflect the monastic ethos of the Mother House which was common in Germany, yet in this country they tended not to live in large institutions and were not members of a religious order.) Their ecclesial status was never fully determined, in particular there were ongoing discussions about whether they were ordained into holy orders. In 1930 the Lambeth Conference described the order of deaconesses in the Church of England as *sui generis* and thus effectively denied that they belonged to the same order as deacons. In 1987, when the majority of deaconesses were ordained to the diaconate it was not a conditional ordination. However, interviews with some of those who were ordained suggests that few saw any difference between their ministries as deaconess or deacon.

As Hall observes, with hindsight we can ask why the Church did not consider reforming the diaconate more radically in the nineteenth century, given the importance then attached to the works of the Greek and Latin Fathers. Instead, the Church of England maintained the medieval attitudes to order and ministry, trying to reconcile them with the new urban context in which it ministered. Hall suggests that the nineteenth century developments of religious and monastic life were essentially pragmatic, in the face of changing contemporary needs and attempts by some gifted individuals to pursue their own visions. The Church of England managed to avoid any attempts to reconcile its own internal Catholic – Protestant tensions or questions of order, and failed to examine the diaconate as a distinctive order of ministry. As a result an exclusively female lay ministry emerged, sharing some features of the diaconate but later declared to be *sui generis*, with roots in church polity and an ecclesial communion (the Lutheran Church in Germany) that was at odds with that of the Church of England. The emphasis of the ministry of deaconesses was initially nursing or education and they became social workers with a church base.

1.5 Caritas and Diakonia

Sven-Erik Brodd from the Church of Sweden, writing in 'The Ministry of the Deacon'[16] draws a distinction between *caritas* and *diakonia*. *Caritas*, charitable work (which may be voluntary and thus a matter of free choice), has been carried out by individual believers or associations of believers including monastic and religious orders, guilds, societies and associations, all of which can be ealizedicd as the sum of their members. *Caritas* is the mark of each Christian. In contrast, *diakonia* is ecclesiological in character, it is not the sum of charitable functions but the deacon exercises charity because it belongs to the functions of the ordained diaconate. Brodd notes that it includes serving at table, thus making the fundamental link with the mystical body of Christ in which all ministries in the church are rooted since the church is founded in the first eucharist. *Koinonia* is expressed in a ministry of love which deacons, together with the whole church, exercise. This includes, but is not defined by, care of the poor. Brodd argues that defining the deacons' ministry as that of care of the poor is a nineteenth century idea (although the Working Party notes that this suggestion needs to be compared with other work, for example that of Collins). This is a particular issue for the churches in Scandinavia where the diaconal ministry often lacks the liturgical element but is instead primarily an arm of social services based in the church.

The significance of the connection of diaconal ministry with service at table lies in the eucharistic meal, to which the *agape* meal was attached in some way, being the centre of the early church. The resulting creation of a sharing, socially responsible community was one expression of *caritas*. The *agape* meal was supervised and headed by the bishop and deacons. Today the *agape* has been subsumed into the eucharistic celebrations, but if it is true that *diakonia* is structural in essence then it is realised in the exercise of the *agape*, which is founded in the eucharist. There is, thus, no room for a purely functional or sociological view of charity and diaconal work, since they have an inherent eschatological dimension. BEM expresses this in paragraph 21, 'the place of (the ministry of deacons and deaconesses) between the table and the needy properly testifies to the redeeming presence of Christ in the world.'

Brodd develops this thinking to explain how, in nineteenth century Germany, the need for a ministry dedicated to charitable works led to the introduction of deacons and deaconesses in a culture that was heavily pietistic and evangelical. Gradually, in this culture, a functional view of office emerged, parallel to the emerging professional view of office based on professional competence. Brodd argues that the idea of role was taken over from psychology, with the danger that ordination could be seen to have no effect since the deacon plays a role which is not integrated into his or her personality. The alternative approach, set out by Brodd, is to recover the early church emphasis on ordination as the prayer for a reception of spiritual gifts, ultimately the Holy Spirit. This changes the perspective from what a deacon does to what a deacon is and to the gifts are given to the deacon in ordination.

2. The Theological Context of Diaconal Ministry: The Working Party

2.1 Old Testament roots of the diaconate

In our discussions we noted that the ministry of the priest is seen as having some roots in the ministry of priests in the Old Testament. This can lead to confusion where the word 'priest' is lifted unthinkingly out of one context into another, but there are also valuable insights to be learned from the Old Testament sources. In general, only the New Testament has been trawled for insights into the ministry of the deacon and we explored the possibility that the ministry of the deacon might also have roots in the Old Testament, even if the word 'deacon' is not used.

If we look for an insight into the nature of God witnessed to by the Old Testament documents, a key concept is that of 'righteousness'. In the story of Tamar (Genesis 38) righteousness is shown to be a term governing relationships and the behaviour appropriate within them. The overlapping concepts of 'justice' and 'law' are drawn in at this point, with particular stress laid on the intertwining of the human and the divine relationships and the social context of righteousness. The concept of righteousness is further illustrated in the wisdom literature, drawing out its presupposition of a given and perceived order within the world and society. The related concept of the divine ordering of the natural world can be seen in Genesis 1, Psalm 19 and Job 38, whilst Psalm 72 illustrates the idea of the king's role in preserving God's order and righteousness in society. Job, together with texts from Ecclesiastes, draws out the mysterious and hidden nature of God's ordering of the world.

Given that humans failed to live in a way that reflects God's righteousness and justice, prophets were called to draw the people's attention back to God. This took them to the edges of society, for some this even meant going into exile with the people away from the former security of Jerusalem. Prophets in the Old Testament were not priests but were deeply concerned with the well-being of the people they were sent to or lived among. They were rooted in their local community – for example Amos was a vinedresser – but were also at times uncomfortable with the culture and thus able to question what was going on and to interpret this in the light of their knowledge of God. Whilst the disturbing and comforting ministry of the prophets is reflected today in the ministry of bishops and priests, we should not lose the strand in Old Testament prophetic ministry that was not necessarily priestly, that stood at times with and among the people and at times on the edges of society, seeing through the veneer and acting on behalf of the poor and oppressed.

If we look at stories in the Old Testament that exemplify aspects of diaconal ministry, we can consider Joseph who was in a servant role wherever he was placed – in prison or in administrative authority. His servanthood drew on his understanding and proclamation of the word of God, by word and deed. The story of Moses depends upon elements of what might be called diaconal ministry, beginning with that of his sister at the time of his birth. When he claimed he could not speak well God provided him with Aaron, his father-in-law persuaded him to delegate some of the practical tasks of providing judgement and justice for the people in their disputes, and Joshua was trained to be his assistant. It is notable that Joshua spent time in the tent after Moses left, suggesting a rootedness in worship that nurtured his ministry of assistance. Samuel, too, combined ministry at the shrine with service to Eli. It is also interesting to consider whether Second and Third Isaiah reflect an understanding of diaconal ministry, particularly where there is reference to the Servant of the Lord and in passages like Isaiah 56 where the theme of the nations being blessed through the people of God is developed. Certainly passages such as Isaiah 61:1-3 point to the later ministry of the deacon in being alongside the poor, the broken hearted, the captive and those who mourn, not only to comfort but to bring God's good news.

Such sources can help us to reflect upon the righteousness of our own communities and to describe the network of relationships there, drawing on both the human and the divine dimensions. The Old Testament asks us to consider the forces that determine the ordering of our community, the groups or individuals responsible for the maintenance of order, those who protest about distortions in society, those who feel there is no order, those who suffer from it and those who work for well-being. The holistic witness of the Old Testament means that we cannot overlook the ecological dimension of our life in community. It also presents us with the question of how we think about diaconal ministry within the network of relationships that we experience, and how our lives reflects God's righteousness.

Another interesting question is whether the ministry of angels as they appear in the Old Testament manifests some of the characteristics of diaconal ministry as we have come to understand it. Angels were servants of God sent by God to act as agents for the well-being of humans or to challenge them with God's message.

2.2 The New Testament, and Collins' work

When we turn to the New Testament we find the word 'deacon' in the epistles, but our understanding of diaconal ministry draws also from other sources, particularly the ministry of Jesus who described himself as 'I am among you as one who serves' *(diakoneō)* (Luke 22:27, see also Luke 12:37). Barnett's survey of the biblical material[17] shows that in its noun form *diakonos* occurs thirty times in the New Testament and carries a range of meanings from menial work to the service of God (Mark 9:35, Colossians 1:23). Paul describes himself and his ministry in diaconal terms, serving the gospel and the church (Ephesians 3:7, Colossians 1:23), he also speaks of some of his co-workers as deacons for God (Colossians 1:7, 1 Thessalonians 3:2). There are also references to the diaconal ministry of the disciples, of certain women and some named men. The concept clearly covered many forms of service, and is described by Barnett as pointing in two directions at the same time – diaconal ministry is first of all sent by God in Christ and therefore has God as its source and reference point, but it also serves others, especially but not exclusively those in the church.

In the early church people were chosen to oversee the service at table in connection with the daily distribution of food to widows (Acts 6). It is clear from later in this chapter that Stephen, one of these people, also preached since it was his words not his service that led to his arrest. The word 'deacon' is not used of them, despite its later application to their ministry by Irenaeus (c185). Instead the word 'deacon' is used in other contexts, often in letters where 'bishops and deacons' are greeted (Philippians 1:1) or where, in the pastoral epistles, 'deacon' is used to refer to an emerging office, particularly in the Hellenistic church which had no presbyters in the early decades, in contrast to the emergence of presbyters in Jerusalem in the fifties.

Barnett can find no prototype in Judaism or pagan religions for the deacons as they emerged in the early church. In classical Greek writings the word has the meaning of servant, messenger or civil official. It is these meanings that Collins has explored. In the General Synod debate, Professor Anthony Thiselton welcomed the report with measured enthusiasm but questioned some of Collins' work, particularly his method of drawing together meanings drawn from the words *diakoneō* and *diakonos* and offloading them onto the office of deacon. In the light of Thiselton's questions, we consulted The Revd. Dr. David Holgate at STETS for his comments. He explained that the problem with using a synthesis of meanings from a range of Hellenistic texts, then overlaying that cluster of meanings on the New Testament, is that authors of texts use words to mean what they expect their hearers to understand by them: 'meanings have words, not words have meanings'. In the Exegetical Dictionary of the New Testament (1990) *diakoneō* refers to service in Greek, without implications of meniality whereas *douleo* does have connotations of subordination. In New Testament usage *diakoneō* refers to apostolic leadership activities marked by charitable service and the proclamation of the gospel. The implications of lowliness and humility come into *diakoneō* from the synoptics where it is redefined by Jesus' own example. In later New Testament texts it refers to the ministry or proclamation of the gospel but the pastoral epistles do not limit the activity of *diakonia* to the office of *diakonos*.

Whilst some scholars might question all Collins' methods because of the danger of retrospective reading back in exegesis, Thiselton recognises the importance, if not the uniquely definitive nature, of Collins' work. Barnett observes that word studies, such as that by Collins, offer some insights but the functions in which the deacons are involved are more determinative. He also accepts that to the extent that Collins is correct in his observations about the narrow definition of *diakonia* as charitable works, the modern conceptualisation of *diakonia* is inadequate. Without accepting that any Christian ministry is menial or servile, Barnett argues that Collins reads contemporary secular values into the words, rather than the spirit and teaching of Christ. He is even more critical of Collins for his reliance upon church structures that appear to be inherited from the medieval period rather than the early church where baptism was the basic sacrament of ministry. Our understanding is that this is a charge of reliance that Collins would refute, but it illustrates the continuing debate among scholars on the diaconate within which churches need to make decisions.

In his later work, most recently 'Deacons and the Church'[18] which was published as our report was being finalised, Collins returns to the exegesis of Mark 10:45 and Acts 6. In the case of the former, 'The Son of Man came not to be served but to serve, and to give his life as a ransom for many', Collins argues that if we take the verse as a whole and do not stop at 'to serve', we see that Jesus' service was directed to the One who had called to him at his baptism and was performed by carrying out the mission to which he had been consecrated. In his discussion of Acts 6, Collins addresses the link between the activities in Acts 6 which have roots in *diakonia* and *diakonein* and the title 'deacon'. In summary, the threads of his argument[19] are that in some sectors of the church, notably those shaped by the teaching of Calvin, Acts 6 has been used to make social work the defining activity of deacons. Collins questions this given that Luke does not mention the word 'deacon' despite his familiarity with all that the *diakon-* words stood for in Greek language, religion and culture. He argues that throughout Acts Luke uses the *diakon-* words for the ministry by which the word of God spread from Jerusalem, initially by the first disciples and then by Paul. He concludes that the ancient audience for Acts would understand Acts 6:1 to mean that the Greek speaking widows were being overlooked in the daily preaching of the Word and, since the Twelve could not leave the public proclamation in the temple, these women needed preachers who could speak to them in Greek, preferably at home when they came together at their tables.

In both these cases, Collins' scholarship suggests that the emphasis of service is not menial service of others but service of God expressed in fulfilling the ministry to which one is called. This contrasts greatly with the emphasis that comes particularly from the Reformation of reading 'service' as 'social work', a theme that we return to later in this report. In our consultations, the Revd. Sue Woan commented that Collins does not explore the Old Testament source for the imagery of 'Christ as servant' and she drew our attention to the New Testament's use of Christ as the fulfilment of the suffering servant character which forms the *raison d'être* for Christians to adopt a servant like attitude. Instead, whilst Collins interprets servanthood in terms of the slave ethos of the times he does not set alongside this the perception of the people of Israel from the time of the giving of the covenant as having a servant role to the nations, typified in the suffering servant character. We summarised our own discussions on the Servant passages briefly in the previous section.

A different but related study is that by Deidre Good[20] on the word 'meek' (*praus*). She is concerned to free the word of distorting connotations of servility and to reclaim its classical meanings which, in relation to animals, is 'tame' and in relation to kingship is the opposite of tyrannical or despotic (thus Herod is the bad example to which Jesus' kingship is contrasted). Jesus is not passive, weak or ineffectual, but stands up to Pilate and overturns the tables of the money changers. She suggests that the contemporary equivalent for meekness might be 'calm, considered, wise, firm, compassionate response.'

There is no suggestion that there is a first century model of diaconal ministry to which we can ascribe 'authority' for diaconal ministry today. For example, in a recent book on the women deacons of the early church, John Wijngaards writes,

> It would be a mistake to imagine that these three functions (*episcopoi*, *presbyteroi*, *diakonoi*) had the same contents that they have for us today. In the course of the centuries so much has changed, with variations between different countries as well, that it is difficult even to summarise the enormous shifts that took place. ... the ministries varied greatly in contents, status and function from place to place and from one era to the next. It would be a mistake to generalise.[21]

In our work we have sought to be faithful to the tradition that we inherit without using any one part of it as an absolute blueprint. Taken overall, it seems to us that, despite some differences of interpretation, the implications of the insights of these various New Testament scholars points to a wider understanding of *diakonos* and *diakonia* than the church has held in the past, and to the need to avoid any emphasis on meniality or passivity, stressing rather the example of Christ himself. The word studies by Collins point us to some dimensions of diaconal ministry that may be significant in broadening our understanding of the diaconate, particularly when they can be set alongside examples from the New Testament and the writings of the early church.

2.3 Theological questions about lay ministries

We have discussed the questions raised by the inadequate theological understanding in relation to lay ministries at the time they emerged, and the potentially confusing heritage that results. This manifests itself, in relation to Readers, in concern that deacons will duplicate or displace Readers and disempower lay people. It was expressed in the debate at General Synod in terms of lack of clarity about overlapping ministry, and the suggestion that most Readers might simply be ordained deacon because the two vocations are so similar. This relies upon a purely functional view of ministry which we believe is inadequate (and – if those purely functional terms are considered - also confuses the focus of the two ministries). If Caroline Headley's points are taken seriously, the significant aspect of Reader ministry is not simply what Readers do but who they are – they are lay people whose ministry placards the ministry of lay people as part of the ministry of the church. Readers make visible the fact that God gives different gifts to different people and that ordination is not the passport to ministry, instead by baptism we are called to share in the ministry of the church. In practical terms, Readers may share some ministry with others – both lay and ordained – but function is not the key issue. If the Church looks solely at function and decides to ordain most of the Readers it will not only violate the strong sense of lay vocation that most Readers feel, but will simply recreate the theological void surrounding the lay ministry of deaconesses.

The language of 'bridge building' is now common in relation to Reader ministry, and has come to be understood as one of its central facets. This is reflected in the choice of 'Bridging the Gap' as the title for the recent book on Reader ministry. However, as noted earlier, this book does not describe or explore the gap. One possibility is the gap between lay and ordained ministry, which is in danger of suggesting that Readers, too, are *sui generis*, and thus open to the uncertainties the deaconesses faced for over one hundred years. However, Headley's emphasis on the ministry of Readers deriving from the fact that they are lay people gives a firm base for Reader ministry, with the emphasis being not on the lack of ordination (and thus what is 'missing') but on the recognition of a ministry of lay people given by training and licensing. In that sense, Readers and deacons can never displace each other, since the ecclesial base of their ministry lies in two complementary facets of the theology of the church's ministry. The more relevant gap, in terms of the ministry of the church, is not between lay or ordained but the gap between what happens in the church building on Sunday morning and what happens during the rest of the week. It is this gap that diaconal ministry and Reader ministry should both be directed towards in their complementary ways. Readers, as theologically trained lay people, do it in all the ways that Headley alerts us to. Deacons, as ordained ministers (whose emphasis may not be on the Reader's ministry of preaching and teaching), do it by holding together ministry in the world and in worship, calling us to worship and sending us out to serve.

It seems to us that if the Church has an adequate theological understanding of the ministry of Readers, and through them makes visible and encourages the ministry of lay people, there can be no conflict with the ministry of deacons whose ordination places them within the threefold order of the church. The problems arise if the emphasis is placed on functional tasks, where there may indeed be complementary overlap (although this is not inevitable), and this is allowed to become the defining issue. The reason this appears to be happening is that the proposal to renew the distinctive diaconate is bringing to the surface the lack of theological understanding of the ministry of Readers that the Church has managed to ignore until now. Headley points to the theological issues in her book, but what is needed is a more thorough explanation of the theology and ecclesiology that underlie the ministry of Readers which has a strong emphasis on being teachers.

It is possible that some Readers who undertake a distinctively pastoral or administrative role, or who are emerging as leaders in their local church, were recommended to become Readers because there was, in practice, no other ministerial path open to them except that of ordination to the priesthood which they knew they did not want. The option of the diaconate as a permanent order was rarely, if ever, offered as a realistic proposal. This continues to this day in too many cases, although we are pleased to note the clear sense of diaconal vocation expressed by some deacons in training in this diocese and the way that the vocations process channeled that vocation appropriately. If Readers do find themselves exercising a more diaconal ministry that may be a reason to discern afresh where their vocation lies, recognising that God may have led them to something new, indeed that a previously unavailable opportunity is now open. The fact that this may apply to a few Readers does not call into question the ministry of most Readers as a distinctive and complementary vocation to the diaconate.

The lack of theological understanding affected the deaconesses in a more obvious way than the Readers. They suffered from the lack of resolution of whether their ministry was a lay ministry or an ordained ministry and whether they were a quasi-monastic order or a parish-based ministry. Various decisions were made at various times, usually in response to pressure from the deaconesses on questions such as whether they had been ordained or not and why in the early days they should not marry. The ecclesiological and theological questions were never considered apart from the pragmatic issues as they arose. When, in 1987, the decisions on the ordination of women meant that the majority of deaconesses could be ordained deacon, a spin-off was that the Church of England virtually lost what had become a significant and recognised lay ministry. The few who were not ordained deacon at this time were prevented not by any questions about their vocation to ordained ministry but mainly because they were divorced or married to a divorced person. Once this issue was resolved by the church in relation to ordination, most were then ordained deacon. A few chose to continue in their original vocation, and in this Diocese we have one deaconess.

Whilst the impetus for the ordination of the deaconesses was the question of the ordination of women, what was left unresolved was the question of what the loss of the deaconesses said about lay ministry. This need not have been an issue had the theological and ecclesiological issues been clear from the start, but the church had never resolved where this lay ministry for women fitted into its overall theology of ministry. This appears to bear the hallmark of a Victorian solution to the question 'what to do with the women?' yet despite the inadequate ecclesiological thinking, deaconesses clearly provided a valued and recognised lay ministry within the church focused on the care of people in need. Reviving the distinctive diaconate highlights these unresolved ecclesiological and theological questions about the ministry of deaconesses in the same way that it highlights the need for further work on the ministry of Readers.

There are just over one thousand Lay Pastoral Assistants in this diocese who have been trained to provide some pastoral care on behalf of the church. This is another facet of the collaborative ministry pattern in this diocese. The new LPA training programme provides a focused introduction to many aspects of pastoral care and some parishes have several LPAs who share in this aspect of the church's ministry. Their pastoral focus complements that of Readers, whose main area of ministry is preaching and teaching. In their pastoral work, LPAs parallel some aspects of the ministry of deacons. In one parish the deacon co-ordinates the ministry of the LPAs and, by serving liturgically, expresses the ministry of the LPAs in worship and affirms its part in the ministry of the church.

It is possible that (like some Readers) some LPAs might have a diaconal vocation. This is not to say that all Readers or LPAs must become deacons, but that we should ask if some of them might have diaconal vocations that emerge from their exiting ministry, can be focused in a new way through ordination and then act as catalysts for all Christian discipleship. Like LPAs and Readers, the deacon inhabits the area of interface with the wider community. Whereas Readers and LPAs are called to an office for which they are blessed and licensed, the deacon is part of the threefold order and is ordained to a lifelong ministry that has a wider remit including agency or ambassadorship as well as practical service.

If we look at Jesus' ministry in the first century we see the example of a permeable membrane between 'religion' and 'world'. Jesus moved with ease and comfort between the two, and was not afraid to critique or commend either. From its early days the church has regarded the deacon as the symbol of the servant ministry of Christ and whilst LPAs and Readers share in this servant ministry, they do not function as symbols of it. Following Christ's example, we should expect to find the deacon as the conduit of discourse between church and world, able to speak and act on behalf of each, working so that this interaction can be extended by others. Earlier in the report we referred to the Old Testament emphasis on God's righteousness and justice; if the church takes this seriously it should act as the agent of God's righteousness and eschatological sign of God's kingdom, facilitating constant discourse between the church and the world. The deacon is uniquely placed to facilitate this discourse as the ordained person who is trained and charged to inhabit the crucial boundary area. Some Readers and LPAs whose more focused lay ministry also takes them regularly into this area may need to be challenged by their parish church, which knows them and the fruit of their ministry, to consider if their vocation is more diaconal. If this is case then the church should test that possible vocation with them. Later in this report we describe the characteristics of diaconal ministry and outline some of the signs that may point to a diaconal vocation. On the other hand, many Readers and LPAS will have a clear ministry to preach and teach or to provide pastoral service as lay people and should not be distracted from that by questions of diaconal ministry.

So far we have considered lay ministries that are licensed by the church. There are also numerous unlicensed ministries that express the varied gifts of church members from flower arranging to church cleaning, Sunday School teaching to care of the churchyard. Thus we discussed whether, in some charismatic churches, the worship leaders might be functioning in a diaconal way as they draw people into worship, incorporate music into the intercessions and perhaps participate in prayer ministry afterwards. In Scandinavia there are examples of musicians being treated on a par with deacons, with state funding to facilitate this. The same might be true of a ministry among young people that takes a youth worker or Church Army Officer out into the neighbourhood, thus sharing in the diaconal ministry of reaching into forgotten corners of the world and seeking out those who have lost their way. Another possibility is the work of parish administration being an indicator of diaconal ministry. In all these cases we are not suggesting that these lay ministries are coterminous with diaconal ministry or automatic signs of a wider diaconal vocation, simply that for some people engaged in them they may be indicative of a potential diaconal ministry that the church can recognise and nurture.

2.4 Overlap of ministries

On the question of overlap of ministries, we want to affirm the positive virtue in overlap and question the assumption that 'tidiness is next to godliness'. Instead, we ask if untidiness might be a more biblical model that recognises that even in the early church there was some overlap between ministries. 'For such a time as this' accepts that overlap is desirable rather than to be eliminated and the questions in the General Synod debate appear to be directed more to uncertainty about where foci and boundaries lie rather than the principle.

At the heart of Trinitarian theology is mystery. We can try to define Father, Son and Holy Spirit and we can identify distinctive characteristics of each Person of the Trinity, but as soon as we try to put them in boxes the dynamic of the Trinitarian mystery is lost. The theological concept of *perichoresis* points us to the truth that there is interpenetration of one Person of the Trinity in another, coinherence without confusion. This tells us that the actions of each Person are always co-operative, that there is a hinterland to the actions of each Person of the Trinity. Thus whilst each may act in a distinctive way, this is never divorced from the other two Persons who are involved in the actions of the other and in the dance of the Trinity (the root of *perichoreuo* is 'to dance around'). Since, by God's grace, we are caught up in the life and ministry of the Trinity we are invited to 'join the dance', be drawn into the mystery. This places the emphasis on the dynamic of the dance and Paul Fiddes[22] points out that in a human dance the partners weave in and out, whereas in the divine dance so intimate is the communion that they move in and through each other so that the pattern is all-inclusive.

We explored other images to help us understand this concept. Whilst they lack the intrinsic dynamism of *perichoresis*, they are nevertheless helpful. The rainbow comprises distinct colours but if we concentrate on one at the expense of the others we lose the rainbow. If we try to demarcate the boundary where, for example, red becomes orange, we will never find it since the point of transition can never be seen. There is a focus to the colour that is revealed in the depth of colour at its heart, but the colour itself is not lost when that depth is lost and it begins to merge with another colour. Alternatively, in photography, when taking a photo of flowers the photographer can either focus on the one, having that in perfect focus so that details can be examined but with the surrounding flowers being out of fcous, or the photographer can stand back and achieve an overview in which all flowers are in focus but details are lost. Both ways of taking photos are valid. An implication of this is that fuzziness has its own value when it is a consequence of focus.

Applying those concepts to our theological thinking about ministry, we begin from the affirmation of the Anglican view of the threefold order of ministry and the importance of various lay ministries. Together, lay and ordained, we are caught up in the dance of the Trinity. This is, in effect, the overview in which the photographer stands back and takes a photo of the field of flowers or the rainbow-gazer sees the whole rainbow with its different colours. On the other hand, we can examine each ministry in more detail which is the equivalent of focusing on one flower or one colour in the rainbow, accepting that others will go out of focus or the precise boundaries will never be found. Stephen Croft[23] gives an account of the threefold order of ministry which maintains the distinctive focus or centre of each order, episcopate, presbyterate and diaconate, but argues that everyone is involved in the others at various stages because, whilst there is a centre or focus, there are also points of contact and overlap with others. This principle applies equally to the overlap between lay and ordained ministries, and between different lay ministries.

We have adopted the shorthand of 'rainbow theology' for this way of looking at the mystery of ministry that is born in the Trinitarian *perichoresis*. We have to live with mystery, holding the clarity of focus that frees us to live with the fuzziness or overlap at the edges. If we refuse the risk of living with overlap at the edges, we will lose the detailed focus too and have to be content with standing back and gazing from afar. We will also lose the opportunities for collaboration and enabling the ministry of others where ministries do overlap. On the other hand, we do need to gaze from afar and see the whole in all its beauty and mystery. There is no one normative way to look either at a rainbow or at ministry. In this report we are trying to hold the diaconate in focus whilst also looking at the whole rainbow or photograph of ministry.

Specifically in relation to diaconal ministry, we listened to an extract from a tape of The Rt. Revd. Tom Ray of the Diocese of North Michigan speaking to the North American Association of Deacons. He explained the focus of diaconal ministry and said that we do not have deacons to do our own deacon's ministry for us but in order to reveal and shine a light on the servant ministry that is already embedded in our lives, often unheralded and unappreciated. The diaconate is a clear window through which to see that ordered ministry is not territorial but instead reveals to us a dimension of the depth of meaning of our own baptism. Deacons are not ordained in order to set them apart into special territory but to reveal to us the serving ministry that has always hallowed our homes, workplace, community and church. The deacon explodes our awareness and understanding of diaconal ministry into a daily ministry; having ordained deacons makes an invisible ministry visible and to be recognised as part of Christ's ministry. We note that this understanding builds a bridge between the distinctive ministries of *caritas* and *diakonia* which Brodd drew (see section 1.5).

Another aspect of overlap is the distinctive relationship between certain ministries. In the New Testament and early church there was a close relationship between bishops and deacons although, as Barnett points out,[24] it is easy to read back into the first and second centuries what we find later. In the very early church the deacons were not so much the assistants of bishops as servants of the church, who at times did assist the bishop but also were dispensers of the church's charities. At this time the bishop was in the local church rather than in a diocese so, until dioceses with a single bishop emerged, the deacons' service to church and bishop were virtually coterminous. By the time of Hippolytus[25] (c215) deacons were ordained to serve the bishop and carry out his commands, they did not take part in the council of the clergy but were to attend to their own duties and to make known to the bishop such things as were needful. In the Epistle of Clement to James[26] (c313–325 but with origins in c160–220) deacons were described as being eyes to the bishop, but they did not work exclusively for him since they were also to bring the needs of the sick 'to the multitude' (i.e. the church). In Syria in the third century bishops had increasing responsibilities and were becoming more remote from the local churches so deacons acted as their intermediaries. The bishop was the focus of unity, the deacons were his eyes and ears in diverse situations. By the end of the fourth century deacons were no longer the bishop's personal staff; presbyters took the place of bishops in the local churches and the deacons became their assistants as well. In the medieval period when the diaconate had become primarily transitional and liturgical, much of the administrative work was carried out by archdeacons.

This relationship between bishop and deacon has obviously evolved in the light of changing circumstances, but in its early form it shows the deacon very much as enabler of the ministry of the bishop and the church. One author[27] has used the image of the deacon as the 'old retainer' servant who knows the family he or she has served for years and uses that knowledge to take the initiative and keep it running smoothly. The deacon in relation to the bishop shows a minister who is a support to another person with a willingness to be in a back-room / servant role that facilitates the more public ministry of the bishop. To fulfil this ministry the deacon does not need to be a priest, but does need to be theologically trained. In this diocese, the ministry of The Revd. Roy Overthrow exemplified this relationship of bishop and deacon, and the accompanying facilitating role of the deacon, and we note that some other dioceses have adopted a similar form of diaconal ministry. Although Roy's ministry was a particular contemporary expression of the relationship between bishop and deacon, the principle is long-established in the church and we will recommend later that this relationship of the bishop with all the deacons is made more visible.

With the emergence of team ministries, a further extension of the relationship of bishop and deacons should be expressed in the deacon being the eyes and ears of the Team Rector or Incumbent who is in the team or benefice in the place of the bishop. From our consultations we know that this is already beginning to happen in some places. It is particularly appropriate in rural areas where the incumbent may live in a different village to the deacon who can be the church's representative person in that area, working with and under the leadership of the incumbent. All good ministry begins in listening and the listening skills of the deacon need to be coupled with skills in interpreting what is heard. To draw from the business world, the best managers have their ear to the ground and in collaborative ministry this can be expressed through different roles and responsibilities rather than in terms of hierarchy. This is another expression of the relationship of the bishop with the deacons and it makes visible the complementarity of the orders of ministry which overlap but have distinctive natures.

Just as antiphonal singing is a conversation in music, and the versicle and response tradition wraps the congregation into the dialogue, so the nature of the church is about 'The Lord be with you … and also with you.' The dialogue between bishop and deacon, priest and deacon needs to be seen as a part of the given of church order and governance. This conversation is expressed as the deacon serves alongside the bishop or priest in a complementary role, reflecting the interface of priestly and diaconal ministry in the liturgy as each takes their part. In contrast to the interplay of priest and deacon in the liturgy, we noted that the relationship between priest and Reader is often expressed differently, particularly in most rural parishes where Readers rarely serve liturgically alongside the priest, but are likely to be leading a service in another parish and thus fulfilling their ministry of preaching, teaching and leading in worship.

2.5 The Nordic Churches

On the question of the diaconate in the Nordic churches, their stress on making proper provision for the exercise of the church's ministry of care is very important. However, given the understanding of ministry in the Church of England, insights from the Lutheran Nordic churches which have a more functional and skills-based view of the diaconate as the church's pastoral care arm need to be interpreted carefully rather than adopted unquestioningly. The diaconate in the Nordic churches bears many similarities to the deaconess movement in the Church of England.

However, the Nordic churches present a particular prophetic challenge to us which requires careful discernment if we ask ourselves questions about the state of our society – in particular the Welfare State - in ten or fifteen years time. Some of the questions we have in mind are where the NHS is going, the implications of the failure of care in the community policies, the increasing numbers of elderly people as baby boomers will soon reach pensionable age, and the implications of events in the world money markets for the provision of services and pensions. These factors should force the Church of England to ask if we need to re-engage with forms of ministry that were once the province of monastic orders and deaconesses, but have been taken over by the welfare state which now finds itself struggling. The challenge to the Church of England is to allow the Nordic churches to be prophetic rather than to provide an historic input, so that we are not governed by their model but learn from it.

We have not reached any conclusions as this debate is one that needs to be conducted in a wider sphere than the working party, but we draw attention to the questions. The Nordic diaconate has tended to be skills-led, attracting people with a professional background in the caring professions and providing them with a venue for their professional work, whereas we believe that the diaconate in the Church of England must be vocation-led whether or not this includes professional skills. However, if we believe that the Church of England needs to respond to changes in secular welfare provision, without simply becoming an arm of the welfare state, then among our deacons there will have to be people who bring appropriate professional skills to their wider diaconal ministry. There will be implications for the encouragement and nurture of diaconal vocations among people with such gifts, but not at the expense of vocations among people who do not have professional skills in the caring professions. Within the theology of ministry that we have in this diocese, such deacons should not – as in the Nordic model – do all the caring work on behalf of the church. Instead, in Bishop Tom Ray's words, they will reveal and shine a light on the servant ministry that is already embedded in our lives, often unheralded and unappreciated, exploding our awareness and understanding of diaconal ministry into a daily ministry, making an invisible ministry visible as part of Christ's ministry.

2.6 *Caritas* and *Diakonia*

Brodd's distinction between *caritas* and *diakonia* can shed some light on the nineteenth century tensions between the high church and the evangelical church in their response to social needs of the day. The high church responded through the church, typically through the 'slum priests' and the newly re-founded religious orders as well as the deaconesses who were attached to parishes and worked under the direction of the priest, whereas the evangelicals responded by founding societies to address specific social ills. As noted in the previous section, the development of the Welfare State and Social Services has removed many responsibilities from the voluntary sector, including churches, whilst the divide between high church and evangelical church has been largely bridged in relation to charitable works. In practical terms the approaches normally complemented each other, but the Church of England never addressed the ecclesiological issues involved.

Christine Hall[28] quotes Yannaras' argument from the Orthodox tradition that deacons need to be ordained because, '…in the church, caring activity is a manifestation of the truth and the actualisation of life, not altruism and utilitarian love for one another.'[29] Put another way, Brodd writes that the fact that the church is a community of love and *koinonia* is the only perspective from which deacons exercise a ministry of love together with the whole church. It is a nineteenth century reversal of this idea that says that deacons' ministry is one of love because they take care of the poor.[30] Brodd also argues that deacons are 'to make the eucharistic *koinonia* more effective, otherwise the risk is that they become signs not of the kingdom of God but of an internal secularisation of the churches.'[31] A recovery of the understanding of the diaconate as having an eschatological dimension gives coherence to the church's ministry to the needy and reinforces the place of the deacon at the heart of the eucharistic worship of the church, sharing in ministry at table with bishops and priests. It also provides a centre for the caring ministry in the church's name that is offered by Lay Pastoral Assistants. Wherever the deacon works with the LPAs this is not only good collaborative ministry but the deacon can give expression in the liturgy to this aspect of the church's ministry, reinforcing its eschatological dimension.

2.7 Theological conclusions: the richness of ministry

We recognize that, at first glance, there may appear to be tension between our desire for an integrated approach to ministry and the seemingly hierarchical context of the Anglican church (as well as the Roman Catholic and Orthodox churches) whereby from the *laos* some are called as deacons, of whom some are called as priests, of whom some area called as bishops. If this ordering is seen not as being about power and status, with increased status the further 'up' the hierarchy one goes, as tends to be assumed in secular organizations, but instead is understood to be about cumulative responsibility for the edification of the church, then the emphasis is on responsibility within the overall ministry of the church, rather than rank or standing. It reminds us too that all ministry is rooted in baptism. If three-dimensional language is to be used, we could say that there is a horizontal dimension of diversity and a vertical dimension of unity in hierarchy, an understanding that accords with the patristic doctrine of the Trinity and with early Christian understandings of authority: 'early Christian egalitarian ecclesiology in no way excludes leadership and authority.'[32]

Drawing together all the insights that have been explored thus far, we want to affirm the importance of the Trinity as the basis for all ministry, ordained and lay. We have in mind the dynamic life and mutual love of the Trinity, but also recognise that at times in its history the church has more specifically identified the threefold order of ministry with the three Persons of the Trinity. For example, in the early church it was understood that deacons represent Christ, just as bishops represent the Father. This insight was lost with the sacrificial emphasis of medieval eucharistic theology when the priest became the representative of Christ because of the specific role of the priest in the mass. In our discussions we observed that at present we have, effectively, a 2.5 fold ministry and we need to bring diaconate into focus if the church is to have the threefold ministry in its fullness. This means that the diaconate is not simply being rescued from being an also-ran or staging post on the way to priesthood, but is restoring the richness of the threefold order of ministry.

In relation to diaconal ministry, the Montreal Faith and Order Conference in 1983[33] (under the auspices of the Faith and Order Commission of the World Council of Churches) noted the recovery of the understanding of the royal priesthood of the whole people of God and that ministry belongs to the people of God by virtue of baptism into the identity of Jesus Christ whose body is the church. *Diakonia* belongs to the whole life of the church and is concretely expressed and embodied in a particular ministry which can serve as a sign of what the church essentially is. The Consultation on Deacons in 1964 concluded that Christ is the Deacon, so by analogy the church is a diaconal body.[34] Deacons are not only instruments but, by virtue of their ordination, are also signs of what the church is. Accordingly, the Lutheran Church of Sweden, where the emphasis of diaconal ministry is on caring service, now sees the main task of deacons as building up and equipping the church so that it can become what it is – the sacrament of Christ to the world. In the Church of England the deacon also has an important liturgical ministry and we suggest that in the liturgy the deacon's importance is not primarily functional (although that ministry is important) but lies in the fact that he or she placards the diaconal nature of the church. The deacon's sacramental representation, which engages the whole Christian community, is indeed acted out in particular practical ways (because the deacon is never an ornament) but primarily proclaims the servanthood of the church. This emphasis on Christ as Deacon complements the emphasis on the priestly ministry of Christ.

It is not possible to derive a specific and defined order of deacons (or indeed any set and fixed order of ministry) from the New Testament to which we can attribute the description 'biblical model'. Nevertheless, the early church, as evidenced by some of its second and third century writings, recognised the ministry of ordained deacons in the period after that described by the New Testament. Although we cannot identify a New Testament blueprint for the diaconate as we know it, we know that from the very early days there was a pattern of call and commission to a particular ministry by prayer and the laying on of hands. Thus we read in Acts 6:7 that the apostles laid hands on the seven for the ministry to which the church had called them, whilst Barnabas and Saul (Acts 13:2-3) and Timothy (1 Timothy 4:14) are also described as having hands laid on them for a particular ministry. We are not suggesting that this implies ordination to the diaconate, but note the information about the practice of the very early church in publicly setting people aside for particular ministries.

We recognise the importance of the biblical and historical studies, as well as their silence on some matters on which we might wish they would speak. In our work we have not found any reason to stall our work on the diaconate in the church today because of differences between scholars on points of detail in the biblical record and historical sources which mean that there is no blueprint. The very lack of a 'blueprint' from the early church is a positive challenge to the church to faithful and creative thinking on diaconal ministry in our own ecclesial tradition and our own time.

In our discussions, not only of the biblical and early church sources, we recognise that all ministry is founded upon that of Christ, that the office of the deacon placards or makes visible Christ's ministry in which all are called to share. Bishop Tom Ray (section 2.4) expresses the deacon's particular expression of our participation in Christ's ministry very vividly. It is important that deacons keep diaconal ministry visible in the church, making it clear that they are not thereby serving on behalf of the church in order to absolve others from their own sharing in the diaconal ministry of Christ, but in order to stir up all Christians to their baptismal vocation.

At the same time, when the church has ordained deacons it has given them particular charges that are an expression of their vocation to a focused participation in diaconal ministry. The wide-ranging discussions on the diaconate keep coming back to themes of the deacon as a person on the boundaries of society, at the door of the church, as hinge at the interface between shrine and street, as go-between. The language of 'bridge builder' has been used in some reports but we have tried to avoid this, not least because it is in danger of being so widely used in relation to a variety of ministries that it becomes meaningless as a description of a distinctive ministry. Whilst the images of door keeper or gate keeper are valuable, perhaps reflecting Benedict's instruction that monastic gate-keepers be older members who are given the role of welcoming and treating all who come as Christ himself, these are quite static images compared to the dynamism inherent in trinitarian life. Therefore we also welcome the insights of the deacon as go-between, ambassador and agent. With reference to Brodd's distinction between *caritas* and *diakonia*, there is no *caritas* involved in being a go-between or ambassador, but there is contact with both 'parties'. In the light of 'rainbow theology', we recognise that this is not exclusive to the deacon, many NSM and MSE priests as well as many Readers share aspects of this ministry through their engagement in their place of work as well as their ministry in the church.

Later in this report we discuss the practical outworking of diaconal ministry. Before we do that we want to affirm the richness of all ministry in the church because this is a sharing in the life of the Trinity. The deacon is a member of the threefold order of ministry within which the deacon's particular contribution is to proclaim the servanthood of the church. This is therefore more than just a functional ministry, (although all diaconal ministry should be practical) because the deacon holds up to the church what it should itself be – a diaconal body since – in the words of the Consultation on Deacons[35] – Christ is the Deacon.

3. The History of the Diaconate in the Anglican Communion

3.1 The Church of England

Before the Reformation, deacons mainly had liturgical and administrative responsibilities. They were bound to celibacy and, whilst a few were permanent deacons, most were ordained priest after a short period as a deacon. 'For such a time as this' describes the situation after the Reformation in this way,

> At the Reformation, the English Church continued uninterrupted the historic threefold ordained ministry; the diaconate remained primarily transitional to the priesthood. Deacons were Clerks in Holy Orders and, at a time when the Eucharist was celebrated only three or four times a year in parish churches and private confession was rare, deacons could perform most clerical functions. Until the Act of Uniformity of 1662, deacons were frequently instituted to benefices. After 1662 bishops tended to ordain men to the diaconate and the presbyterate on the same day, or within a few days, in order to license them to the sole charge of a parish, either as incumbents or as curates serving on behalf of an absent incumbent.[36]

There was, however, a group of clerks who remained deacon for long periods, or permanently: they were the academics who were fellows of colleges, ecclesiastical lawyers, and royal servants engaged in demanding work of administration and diplomacy – people with a specialised function that was thought difficult to combine with the full ministerial obligations of the priesthood.[37] It is interesting to note this as a comparison with John Collins' work on the meaning of diakonia in secular usage: that the primary meaning centres around message, agency and attendance. It may also be put alongside the view of some Methodists that the diaconate may be seen as a specialist ministry, working in particular spheres of expertise and need rather than in general ministry, and with the way in which the Roman Catholic diocese of Evreux, France uses its deacons, to which we refer later. There are also parallels with the Nordic model.

In the nineteenth century, with the emergence of a new sense of professionalism among the clergy and growing awareness of huge pastoral needs in large urban parishes, the diaconate as then understood was taken more seriously. This was a welcome recognition that ordination must include service, but one consequence was that the diaconate came to be seen as a probationary year during which the apprentice priest learned his professional duties rather than a recognition of distinctive gifts of service. However, the development of the deaconess orders at this time pointed to the possibilities of a distinctive diaconal ministry although in practice it emerged as a lay ministry.

The Order of Deaconesses was revived in the Church of England in 1862; by 1917 about a dozen deaconess institutions or houses were established. We have already referred to the ambivalence about whether deaconesses were ordained and whether they were a quasi-monastic order. In the early twentieth century there was a blur between them and accredited lay workers which was never resolved, except that the order of deaconesses was seen as something distinctive. It was only in 1973, with the revision of Canon D1, that deaconesses were allowed to undertake the customary diaconal role in the Eucharist, as well as to officiate at baptisms, funerals and the Churching of Women. A few years previously they had been allowed to preach at public worship, provided it was not at the Holy Communion, although they had previously been permitted to read Morning and Evening Prayer.

In 1974 a report by the Advisory Committee for the Church's Ministry failed to find a convincing theological rationale for the diaconate and recommended abolishing it. The 1976 Anglican Consultative Council disagreed with the report, and in 1977 the General Synod declined to follow its recommendation. The House of Bishops of the General Synod commissioned further work in 1986, resulting in the 1988 report 'Deacons in the Ministry of the Church'. This report recommended that the Church of England make provision for, and encourage, men and women to serve in an ordained distinctive diaconate.

In 1987 some 700 women were ordained as deacons, and in 1994 many women deacons were ordained as priests. The work and debate surrounding these two events overshadowed the follow up of the 1988 report, and only the dioceses of Portsmouth and Chichester carried forward the report's proposals to encourage a distinctive diaconate. As a consequence of the ordination of women, however, the order of deaconess was closed to new applications. Thus the Church of England lost an active order for lay people.

By the mid 1990s, development in ecumenical theology, changes in society, an enhanced missiological awareness, developments in lay ministry and new theological insights based on New Testament research, called for a fresh appraisal of the diaconate. Following a motion from the Ely Diocesan Synod, General Synod requested the House of Bishops to set up a working party on a renewed diaconate, taking these points into account. The working party presented its report 'For such a time as this – a renewed diaconate in the Church of England' to General Synod in November 2001. The report was received and, after debate, was referred to the Ministry Division for further work. In doing so, the Synod altered the remit of the original working party. However, since the report was received by the Synod, it is in the public domain and any Bishop may take forward its proposal that the diaconate be restored as a distinctive, permanent ministry for some ordained ministers and as the fundamental commissioning of all ordained ministers.

3.2 The Anglican Communion

The question of reviving a distinctive diaconate has been aired at various times within the Anglican Communion. In 1958 the Lambeth Conference recommended,

> That each province of the Anglican Communion shall consider whether the office of deacon shall be restored to its primitive place as a distinctive order in the Church, instead of being regarded as a probationary period for the priesthood.[38]

In 1968 the Lambeth Conference took this further and recommended,

- that the diaconate, combining service of others with liturgical functions, be open to:

  - men and women remaining in secular occupations

  - full-time church workers

- those selected for the priesthood

- that ordinals should, where necessary, be revised:

  - to take account of the new role envisaged for the diaconate;

  - by the removal of reference to the diaconate as an "inferior office";

  - by emphasis upon the continuing element of *diakonia* in the ministry of bishops and priests.

The 1984 Anglican Consultative Council resolved that among other topics 'Reviewing the Diaconate' should be studied in the Provinces in 1985-1988 in preparation for the 1988 Lambeth Conference. That Conference took note of developments in different parts of the Communion and said,

> We are confident that there is a need for a more credible expression of the diaconate. We need to rediscover the diaconate as an order complementary to the order of priesthood rather than as a merely transitional order which it is at present. We should ensure that such a diaconate does not threaten the ministry of the laity but seeks to equip and further it. Such a diaconate, furthermore, would serve to renew the *diakonia* of the whole Church: laity, deacons, priests and bishops.[39]

The 1998 Lambeth Conference mentioned the diaconate within the theme 'Called to be faithful in a plural world':

> Where deacons exercise their special ministry within the Church, they do so by illuminating and holding up the servant ministry of the whole Church and calling all its members to that ministry.

> ...renewed attention to the order of the diaconate raises questions about its relationship to the Church and the other orders with which its ministry is carried out. While deacons have traditionally been responsible to the bishop, the nature of their ministry often places them at the intersection between the Church and the broader society in which they serve.[40]

The Conference then asked a number of questions:

> …How, in the varied settings represented within our Communion, can the relationship between servant-ministry and sacramental worship be clarified? How are we to understand the relationship between the ministry of deacons and priests as they serve to build up Christ's Body? How is the work of deacons on behalf of the church in the world drawn into and reflected in the life of the church and its member congregations?[41]

Within the Anglican Communion the situation with distinctive deacons varies. The Episcopal Church of the USA has a considerable number of men and woman deacons, many of whom see this as their permanent ministry. In ECUSA, deacons have four main responsibilities in addition to their specific liturgical ministries. They are carriers of the sacrament, and ministers of prayer and pastoral care to the sick and housebound; providers of social care on behalf of the Church; promoters of social action, engaged with civil society; and agents of the diocesan bishop for special ministries. The question of a transitional diaconate alongside a distinctive diaconate, and of the possibility of direct ordination to the presbyterate, is on the agenda of the House of Bishops of ECUSA but the latter is not a pressing issue.

'For such a time as this'[42] reports that the need for a distinctive diaconate is increasingly being recognized in the Anglican Church of Canada. There are also distinctive deacons in New Zealand, whose ordination rite include the reminder that deacons in the Church of God serve in the name of Christ, and so remind the whole Church that serving others is essential to all ministry. The Anglican Church in Australia (and the Uniting Churches of Australia) have now incorporated the diaconate of women and men as part of their ordained ministries: they are parish and liturgy-based, even when they are working in schools or other institutions. The Church of the Province of South Africa is now committed to introducing a distinctive diaconate, and has revised its ordination rites accordingly, emphasizing the retention of the three-fold ministry and describing the deacon as one who represents the Church in the service of all who need its help.

4. The History of the Diaconate in Other Churches

4.1 The Roman Catholic Church

Within the Roman Catholic Church since Vatican II there has been provision for a distinctive diaconate for men as a ministry of liturgy, word and charity. The language of the documents issuing from the Roman Catholic Church still speaks in terms of 'hierarchy' of ministry with the diaconate as a 'lesser rank'[43] or deacons as 'in the lower grade'[44] Those who are called to the diaconate become the permanent and committed 'servants of the mysteries of Christ and the Church.'[45] In terms of what deacons do, the Roman Catholic Church expects that,

> Deacons…should strive to transmit the word in their professional lives, either explicitly or merely by their active presence in places where public opinion is formed and ethical norms are applied – such as the social services or organizations promoting the rights of family or life…They may be entrusted with the service of charity in Christian education, in training preachers, youth groups and lay groups; in promoting life in all its phases and transforming the world according to the Christian Order.[46]

This is a slightly different understanding of the diaconate in that it includes reference to Christian education and training preachers (which presupposes they are trained to preach), and thus appears to embrace aspects of the ministry of Readers in the Church of England. In 1998 there were just over 24,000 deacons in the Roman Catholic Church. Most men ordained to the diaconate in the Roman Catholic Church are married, and the support of the family is required. However, where a deacon is widowed after ordination, he is not allowed to marry again. This highlights the almost universal lack of clarity about the diaconate since the prohibition on remarriage after bereavement appears to be borrowed from the Orthodox Church and superimposed upon the already slightly ambiguous Roman Catholic position of whether or not ordination requires celibacy. There is also some confusion between their ordination of deacons and the practice that the appropriate dress is normal civilian attire and not a clerical collar and clergy suit of the priest. The reason given for this is that the deacon fulfils his ministry 'in the world, in the street, in his place of work,'[47] but it appears to dilute any visible representative ministry the deacon might have as an ordained person.

In England, where there were 423 Roman Catholic deacons in 1999, deacons tend to be assistants to the priest, whereas in France the deacon has a wider ministry outside parochial boundaries. The diocese of Salisbury has a link with the Roman Catholic diocese of Evreux in northern France, and we would do well to look there for some good practice. The deacons there each have their own individual *mission* according to the needs of their communities and their own gifts and skills. A *Lettre de Mission* is read out at the ordination of the deacon and is signed by the bishop. Some ministries are quite specific: for example, work with immigrants and refugees, work with baptism families, marriage preparation, care for the elderly, diocesan communication, work with unemployed people, rural issues. On the whole, deacons keep to their specific mission without crossing into other ministries or tasks. They see their ministry as quite distinct from that of the priest. Many have a ministry that is very much "hands on". Some of these slightly different method of working might be worth trying in a Church of England diocese where a deacon brings specific skills to his or her ministry or is ministering in a situation where there are specific needs.

'For such a time as this' noted that in the Roman Catholic Church the ministry of deacons has developed permissively in proportion to the enthusiasm of diocesan Bishops for this ministry. Certainly that has happened in England and also in France. It might be that the Church of England will move in the same way; some diocesan Bishops will wish to move forward and encourage the diaconate in their diocese, others will not. The Diocese of Salisbury is in a good position to take a lead on this issue, to be a pioneering diocese, and – without accepting their hierarchical understanding of ministry – the experience of the Roman Catholic Church should encourage us to move ahead as is appropriate in our situation.

4.2 The Lutheran tradition

The strong Lutheran tradition of *diakonia* has referred primarily to the Church's social outreach, often from an institutional base. As seen in the example of the Nordic churches, the ministry of deacons is sometimes exclusively pastoral, rather than blending that ministry with teaching and assisting with the sacraments. The diaconate is a flexible ministry and within the Lutheran tradition deacons may or may not be ordained. Some Scandinavian Protestant churches are beginning to suffer from decreasing funding for institutional *diakonia* and the salaried staff that this requires. This development can make the parochial role of deacons all the more important. From an Anglican point of view, there is considerable ambiguity in the office of deacon in some Lutheran churches. There is currently widespread debate among Lutherans about the ministry of deacons.[48]

The Church of Norway, for example has been wrestling with the issue of whether deacons are within the *ministerium ecclesiasticum*, together with the pastors and bishops, or whether they are to be grouped with cantors and catechists outside the *ministerium ecclesiasticum*. Interestingly, all these ministries are commissioned or ordained by the same basic rite. In 1994, the General Synod of the Church in Norway decided that the biggest of their parishes must have both a catechist and a deacon, calling on the government to grant the necessary finance. The deacon is employed by the local church district board which receives finance from state government, the local commune, church offerings and contributions from members. Most have prior professional training, usually in the areas of health, social studies or education. The deacon is seen as having the distinct task of enabling the people of God to exercise their baptismal discipleship of prayer and care for those in need. The deacon is in charge of the diaconal work in the parish with the main task of planning and promoting the care of others, and encouraging community spirit, particularly in respect of those in need.[49]

The Church of Sweden, on the other hand, has a more clearly defined threefold ministry and, during the 20th century there has been a shift towards seeing the diaconate as an ordained ministry. Since 1999, its deacons have had equivalent canonical status to that of priests though their liturgical role tends to be rather minimal. As in the Church of Norway, candidates must have professional training before being accepted into diaconal training. Indeed, in the 1950s the Swedish government integrated the church's charitable work into the public welfare system. This left the church with work that was complementary and alternative to the welfare provided by the state. The majority of deacons have full-time posts, employed by the local parish or pastoral council. In recent years, the church has been reconsidering its understanding of the ministry of deacons and now recognizes that *diakonia* is not merely optional voluntary service, but belongs to the core of the church's being. Preaching is not only verbal, but must be acted out in service. New ordination rites flow from a growing acceptance of a profile for deacons that includes social work, education in parishes and a new role in the liturgy, and to equip the church so that it can become what is – the sacrament of Christ to the world. The diaconate is always permanent – there are no transitional ordinations.[50]

The Evangelical Lutheran Church of Finland has deacons, most of whom are women, most qualified in nursing although some are qualified in social work. They are backed by substantial government resources and have a prominent place in church and society. However, there is ambivalence about the nature of their ministry: they are not officially recognized as ordained. Over the last few decades, following changes in public healthcare and social welfare legislation, diaconal work has moved away from healthcare and economic issues towards the creation of aid networks, pastoral care and recreational activities. There is also a growing concern for human rights at an international level. Official posts in parishes are only filled by trained deacons. Those with a diaconal vocation must also be qualified in nursing or healthcare (if a deaconess) or social work in the public sector (if a deacon). More deacons are trained than are needed by the church, so they may be employed and paid by hospitals or welfare organizations. Parishes with several deacons can appoint a head deacon; all diocesan secretaries are deacons. Most would see their calling/profession as life-long. In recent years, however, there has been concern that diaconal work has been narrowed to charitable works at the expense of catechetical and liturgical roles. Recent discussion has explored the suggestion that the diaconate is part of 'one ministry' with two possibilities: ministry of word and sacrament, or ministry of word and service.[51]

It can be seen from the experience in these Scandinavian countries that the Lutheran Churches there are faced with questions about the nature of the diaconate. These include the question of whether the diaconate primarily has a social / welfare function fulfilled in close co-operation with, and at least partly funded by, the state, or whether the diaconate is more integrated with the whole life of the church including its worship. Allied to this are questions about whether deacons minister on behalf of the church or whether they facilitate the ministry of all members of the church. The high standards of professional training expected of deacons are an example to other churches, but they also raise the question of whether professional skills are a pre-requisite for a diaconal vocation.

4.3 The Reformed tradition

Deacons have had a secure place in the Reformed tradition since John Calvin made them one of his four kinds of minister: pastors and teachers, elders and deacons. Like Luther, Calvin took the Seven appointed in Acts 6 as the prototype of deacons. 'Conversations on the way to unity 1999-2001' (a report of informal conversations between the Church of England, the Methodist Church and the United Reformed Church [URC]) notes that towards the end of the 16th century, elders were tending to assume the functions of deacons in relation to the poor. This model of eldership is integral to the URC practice today, and they are ordained by the local congregation to a ministry of shared leadership, pastoral care, and the equipping of the people of God.

The United Reformed Church began a ministry of Church Related Community Work in 1981. This has some parallels with some aspects of diaconal ministry in the Church of England, although there is no liturgical or catechetical role. The emphasis is on community work and on enabling people to work on their own problems, hopes and opportunities. A Church Related Community Worker (CRCW), of which there are about 10-12 at any one time, works in partnership with the church and is not 'involved with the local community as a lone person working on behalf of the church.'[52] The URC envisages that having a CRCW will be as much about church development as community development. CRCWs are trained professionally, their training includes long term community placements and attendance at the Partnership for Theological Education in Manchester. Once qualified, CRCWs are not ordained but are commissioned to an accredited church-in-community: a church or group of churches that has successfully applied and been approved for a 5 year project. The 5 year term can be extended for a further 5 years. CRCWs are stipendiary ministers, equal colleagues with ministers of Word and Sacrament.

The Church of Scotland, which is Presbyterian in its polity, has both male and female deacons, generally serving in either disadvantaged urban or remote rural parishes. A liturgical role is not normally involved. The focal point of diaconal ministry in the Church of Scotland is service. The Church of Scotland is currently considering whether deacons should be ordained rather than commissioned.

The Presbyterian Church (USA) has ordained deacons who have a ministry 'to those who are in need, to the sick, to the friendless, and to any who may be in distress both within and beyond the community of faith'. But there is also a modest liturgical role. Deacons may lead the people in worship through intercession, reading the Scriptures, presenting the gifts of the people and assisting with the Lord's Supper.

4.4 The Methodist Church

The Methodist Church of Great Britain, with which the Church of England is moving towards a new relationship through the Formal Conversations and growth in fellowship at every level of the life of the churches, has a diaconate that is distinct from the presbyterate. It is both an order of ministry and a religious order with a rule of life and a community ethos. The Methodist diaconate, which was re-opened in 1986, is not defined especially as a ministry of word and sacrament. However, deacons may assist with the distribution of Holy Communion and preside at the sacrament of baptism. Although they are not required to be Local Preachers, many are and regularly preach and lead worship. The Methodist Diaconal Order has promoted much theological reflection with its members. In May 1999 there were 106 active deacons including 20 probationers, 122 retired and 20 in formation.

Deacons work in a variety of situations: some closely linked to congregations, others in the wider community. A very small number are in secular employment (or 'other appointments'). Pastoral care, mission, teaching, encouragement and enabling can form part or all of their ministry. Many serve in difficult housing estates where the wide variety of their ministry depends upon the local needs. Methodist deacons see themselves positioned primarily at the doorway rather than the pulpit, font or table and believe that this makes a subtle difference to their practice of pastoral care. Deacons share involvement in Holy Communion, preparing the table, receiving the gifts, serving, incorporating intercessory prayers, extending the table to those at the edges, and (in churches that have an Easter Vigil) carrying the paschal candle into church as the sign of sharing in the darkness but keeping faith that it cannot overwhelm the flickering candle – witnessing to resurrection hope and helping people discover or maintain that hope even though 'society' has given up on their neighbourhood or life. One describes her ministry as 'service of Christ, *in* and *through* the church (not 'to'), *with* fellow Christians (not 'to' or 'for') to the world.'[53]

Membership of a Religious Order is a distinctive contribution of the Methodist Church in Britain. This is valued by Methodist deacons because of the depth and quality of their belonging together. Methodist deacons are both an order of ministry and a religious order, and they resist attempts to separate out the two dimensions since together they integrate the active and contemplative dimensions of their vocation. Because deacons work in isolated and marginal situations they depend upon the strong sense of solidarity and mutual support that the Religious Order provides.

A presbyter presides at the ordination of deacons but a deacon shares in the laying on of hands, in order to symbolize the continuity in the diaconate. Ministers (presbyters and deacons) are understood to have a representative ministry, and some recent statements have spoken of the ordained (particularly bishops) being signs of the continuity of the church and the gospel. Both presbyters and deacons are seen as participating in the worship, learning and caring, service and evangelism of the church, but each with a particular complementary emphasis. Words used of deacons include 'leading, extending, connecting and embodying.'[54] Methodist presbyters are not first ordained deacon but are ordained directly to the presbyterate. The report 'An

Anglican – Methodist Covenant 2001' suggests that the latest Church of England report may give fresh impetus to the diaconate as a distinctive ministry, but adds there seems to be a need for further theological convergence on the diaconate.

The United Methodist Church in the United States describes deacons as

> Persons called by God, authorised by the church, and ordained by a bishop to a lifetime ministry of Word and Service to both the community and the congregation in a ministry that connects the two. Deacons exemplify Christian discipleship, create opportunities for others to enter into Christian discipleship, and connect the needs and hurts of the people with the church:
>
> • in the world, the deacon seeks to express a ministry of compassion and justice and assists lay persons as they claim their own ministry; and
>
> • in the congregation, the ministry of the deacon is to teach and form disciples, and to lead worship together with other ordained and lay persons, considering the needs and hurts of the people with the church.[55]

It is interesting to note the emphasis placed on the deacon's ministry, whilst shared with others and creative of opportunities for others to grow in discipleship, being shaped by the needs and hurts of the people as though that is the specific diaconal filter for a much wider ministry.

As we were finalising this report, a book on the Ministry of a Deacon in the Methodist Church in the Castleford Circuit was published.[56] Much of the book is specific to that circuit, but some of the experiences and issues have broader application not only to the Methodist Diaconal Order but also to other denominations, despite our different ecclesiologies. Of particular interest to our own study and the relationship of deacon and priest in a parish or team, the reflection from the Castleford experience is that where the deacon is called upon to undertake the presbyter's role and function the diaconal ministry is overshadowed. This creates stress for the deacon as he or she still desires to fulfil their diaconal vocation, devalues the diaconal ministry and diminishes the congregation's ability to understand and accept different perspectives on ministry. Because of conflicting needs and demands on time, a deacon given pastoral care of churches cannot hope to fulfil a community role in the same situation any more than a presbyter can. Therefore, the book states that ideally the deacon should work in partnership with a presbyter.[57]

4.5 The Orthodox Churches

The Orthodox Churches have retained the diaconate to a greater degree than either the Roman Catholic or Anglican Churches, but the diaconate has ceased to have any charitable functions; instead it is primarily a liturgical ministry in the Eucharist where the deacon has particular responsibilities assigned to him. Deacons may be selected because of their ability to sing the liturgy. Many deacons see their vocation as life-long, although the order is also transitional, with transitional deacons frequently spending several years in the diaconate before ordination as priests. There are examples of deacons sharing in the pastoral and administrative work of the church, but this is not common. There appears to be some interest in the Orthodox Churches for a renewed diaconate – indeed one in which women may have a place. The Inter-Orthodox Theological Consultation of 1988 declared:

> The apostolic order of deaconess should be revived. It was never altogether abandoned in the Orthodox Church though it has tended to fall into disuse…Such a revival would represent a positive response to many of the needs and demands of the contemporary world in many spheres. This would be all the more true if the Diaconate in general (male as well as female) were restored in all places in its original, manifold services (*diakonia*) …it should not be solely restricted to a purely liturgical role or considered to be a mere step on the way to higher 'ranks' of clergy.[58]

Proclamation for a deacon is thus chiefly in lifestyle and example, and formal preaching may not necessarily form part of his/her regular ministry. There will be exceptions to this in certain pastoral situations and where the deacon has strong preaching skills. For this reason, preaching skills should be included in the initial training process so that the deacon is equipped for whatever preaching is part of their ministry.

The catechetical role may include Sunday School work or oversight, and providing a link between those who teach children on a Sunday and the inclusion of children into parish worship. Ministry to families leads naturally into the teaching provided before baptism and confirmation, and also the admission of children to Holy Communion before confirmation.

Where a Reader serves alongside a deacon within a ministry team, particular care will be needed in defining roles and responsibilities and acknowledging each other's ministry. The role of all lay people in teaching and caring must not be devalued — deacons will be enablers and encouragers, listening, observant of the vocations of others.

6.4 The pastoral ministry of the deacon

The deacon's pastoral role in the parish will be pivotal. Roles and responsibilities will vary according to circumstances, and will need to be clearly defined within the ministry team. In a team or parish with a large number of LPAs the deacon will be a facilitator and encourager, enabling LPAs in their ministry. Pastoral work, visiting and building contact with the local community will be seen as vital in taking the gospel to those who will respond to a personal approach. 'Loving concern and practical support are the best ambassadors of the gospel in a largely post-Christian culture.'[73]

The pastoral role will include[74]:

- having a special care and concern for the sick, the disadvantaged, the lonely and those in need within the parish; in rural areas this will involve travel to hospital, old people's homes, mental hospitals, prisons and hostels;

- encouraging and co-ordinating LPAs and all other lay people engaged in pastoral concerns, providing them with the necessary resources and access to further training for the continuation of their work;

- being aware of movements in and out and around the parish, providing continuity and stability; being the 'eyes and ears' of the Incumbent, particularly in rural areas;

- 'searching out the careless and indifferent' (ASB Ordinal), going into parts of the community as yet untouched and building confidence in the work and mission of the church;

- having a special concern for families and the young — in their homes, in the community or places where they meet (crèche, nursery school etc), providing opportunities for them to meet in a Christian context both mid week and within appropriate Sunday worship;

- serving as Chaplain to hospital, nursing home, college or school;

- becoming a focal person in collaboration with the parish priest and ministry team, within a particular geographical area of a multi-parish benefice (perhaps where the deacon happens to live).

6.5 The deacon and administration

There will be deacons who have an administrative gift and who will use it within their "servant" role. This is not a reason for ordaining as deacon all those who are administrators in any parish, benefice or deanery. It is to be seen as an appropriate strand of the vocation of a deacon, and may lead to an enhanced local role, or within a diocesan, charity or community organisation. Good and efficient administration enables others to fulfill their ministry better. As an example of this, we refer to the ministry of the Revd. Roy Overthrow as Bishop's Deacon.

6.6. Summary

The deacon will be the doorkeeper within the parish — one who brings people in and sends them out — who welcomes, cares, listens and follows them up. Deacons link worship on Sunday with work on Monday, and take the gospel out into all the parish. The deacon will enable others in the church both visibly and discreetly, in their mission and ministry, encouraging, serving, quietly gossiping the gospel, and getting into the corners that others cannot reach.

Deacons are accountable to their incumbent and to their bishop; this responsibility comes to them through the recognition of vocation, ordination and the commitment to initial and continuing training. Deacons have a public and ordained ministry that, even if looked at simply in terms of tasks, does not diminish the ministry of the many lay people who have the skills and the calling to do many of these same tasks very competently, efficiently and sensitively. Instead the ordained ministry of the deacon complements the lay ministry of so many other people: ideally all will be working with the encouragement of the incumbent and parish as members of a team, using their gifts for the glory of God in that place. Similarly, the ministry of the deacon complements that of priests and bishops since, by virtue of the fact that they too are ordained deacon, the distinctive deacons hold up to them the vocation they have not left behind when subsequently ordained priest or bishop. At the same time, because the distinctive deacons do not bear the additional ministerial responsibilities of the priestly or episcopal vocation, they are free to devote themselves entirely to diaconal ministry in a way that complements the other ordained ministries. This is particularly relevant to the Methodist Church's experience referred to earlier in this report (Section 4.4), that if a deacon is asked to undertake the presbyter's ministry - something that is possible in exceptional circumstances by special dispensation in the Methodist Church - the distinctiveness of the diaconal ministry is lost because the congregation's needs (not least the resulting time spent in sermon preparation) tend to squeeze out the time for diaconal ministry in the world beyond the church door.

An important element of diaconal ministry in enabling the ministry of others is identified from the Methodist Church's experience. Thus Aitchison writes, 'In 1 John 4:19 it says, "we love because he first loved us". A congregation that does not feel loved will find it difficult to offer love. A deacon, called to represent Christ who serves, has a clear responsibility to enable the congregation to feel loved so that she or he can enable them to love.'[75] The deacon, in his or her ministry, encourages and facilitates the ministry of others by representing and embodying the love of Christ not only to those outside the church, but to those within. Within the Anglican Church, the holistic liturgical, catechetical and pastoral ministry of the deacon should all be directed to this end.

6.7 Some implications: do deacons baptise? do deacons anoint the sick in hospital? do deacons preach?

Throughout this report we affirm the threefold order of ministry in the Anglican Church, and the particular focus of each order of ministry. In so doing we have described diaconal ministry as one that inhabits the boundary areas where church and world overlap and the deacon, in the name of the church, engages with the reality of life for people both inside and outside the church. The deacon, in the ASB Ordinal, is charged with searching out the careless and the indifferent, a charge which is not repeated when deacons are ordained priest. We have also described diaconal ministry as one that stands on the threshold of the church and, by welcoming them and bringing their concerns on their behalf into the heart of the church's life, helps people to cross over what can seem a formidable barrier.

It is almost inevitable that this borderline ministry has an impact for the church where pastoral needs meet church order. One manifestation of this is pastoral ministry with those who are at transitions in their life or on the threshold of the church: baptisms, marriages and funerals are concerned with how people come into and go out of church, a primary focus of the deacon's ministry. They are given liturgical form in the pastoral offices and the sacrament of baptism and also involve a ministry of preparation and 'aftercare'. Preparation for these pastoral offices is a valid part of the deacon's ministry; the area which has not always been clear is the extent of the deacon's involvement in the subsequent liturgy.

To put this in a wider context, deacons may prepare people for marriage and take part in the marriage service itself but, because the marriage involves a blessing, that part of the service is reserved for the priest as part of the priestly ministry of blessing. Deacons can and do conduct funeral services as an appropriate pastoral liturgical provision for the bereaved whom the deacon may know well through visiting. In the Diocese of Evreux, France, at least one deacon takes this even further and expresses his ministry by preparing the body for burial and then conducting the funeral. But does the same apply to the other rite of passage that begins people's life in the church, baptism? Having accompanied a family by preparing them for the baptism of their child, does the deacon baptise – thus completing liturgically what has been begun pastorally and thereby bringing the child / family over the threshold and into the church? The ASB Ordinal refers to baptism as part of the deacon's ministry when the deacon is required to do so, whilst the Book of Common Prayer refers to them baptizing in the absence of a priest. We note that deaconesses baptised as part of their ministry, as did female deacons before 1994 and that Roman Catholic deacons do baptise as part of their ministry. On the other hand, does the deacon continue in the accompanying role and stand alongside those involved as the bishop or priest baptises? If the latter, then the deacon who has been alongside these people in their journey to this point should have some part in the presentation of the candidate for baptism, and the role of the priest or bishop needs to be made clear to the family in terms of a theology of ministry that they can understand. In our consultations we heard from deacons who felt strongly that they should be able to baptize those whom they had prepared.

In the case of baptism, historically deacons shared in the preparation of the candidate and in their baptism, prior to leading them into the church to be welcomed by the church and anointed by the bishop who would later provide post-baptismal instruction. Over the years the immersion and the welcome have been merged and the deacon's role in the first part of baptism has been given to the priest, whilst confirmation at a later date has replaced the post-baptismal anointing by the bishop. We ask the question about who is the church's representative person here where the deacon has been the catalyst for the person to be brought to baptism, has provided the baptism preparation in the name of the church and has brought the person to baptism. Just as in the early church the deacon would baptise, it may be appropriate today for the deacon to complete his or her role as representative minister who has accompanied a person in their journey over the threshold of the church. As with the other situations we have discussed in this section, this would be the liturgical expression of diaconal ministry that has brought a person into the church and to baptism.

We have sought advice on this from a liturgist, particularly in the situation where there is a deacon and a bishop or priest present. Without placing the deacon in the president's role, the possibility of the deacon who has had this pastoral and preparatory role sharing in the baptismal liturgy with the president can be considered. Where the president's role is clearly marked out, so that he or she examines the candidates and anoints with the oil of chrism, the deacon might present the candidates, sign them with the cross and dip them in the water, thus leading them into the church. This would be a good example of a diaconal ministry complementing the presidential ministry of the bishop or priest, modelling the mutuality of ministry that flows from the life of God who is Trinity. This reflects the recommendation in the 1987 discussion document on the Liturgical Ministry of Deacons.[76] Additionally, where a priest is not available, the deacon should baptise those for whom he or she has been providing pastoral and catechetical ministry. In both cases, it models the completion of a phase of the deacon's threshold ministry of welcoming individuals into the life of the church.

Another question that has emerged is the question of anointing the sick whom a deacon visits as part of their diaconal ministry, particularly where the sick person regards the deacon as the 'face of the church'. This is a very significant issue for deacons in hospital chaplaincy but can also arise in the parish. In some Anglican churches, for example in the USA, deacons do, in appropriate circumstances, anoint as part of their ministry of caring for the sick and we are aware that, for pastoral reasons, some deacons in the Church of England do because it seems appropriate in that particular situation at that particular time. The oil has been consecrated by the Bishop and is being applied, and parallels could be drawn with the distribution of communion from the reserved sacrament. As with baptism, a case can be made that, by anointing, the deacon is holding together the pastoral and liturgical ministries of the church and exemplifying diaconal ministry. In saying this, we are mindful of the fact that, whilst normally priests hear confessions and pronounce absolution, occasionally a person may make an informal confession in the presence of a deacon as part of the pastoral encounter. Some Anglican churches make provision for such a situation by providing the deacon, or any other lay person, with an alternative to the absolution given by the priest. The question here is a whether the boundary problem with anointing the sick is substantively different from that of having someone confess their sin (not in the formal sense of 'hearing a confession') and providing assurance of that God does indeed forgive sin. We have already acknowledged that deacons live on the boundary, so it should not be surprising that these questions arise and they need theological underpinning that affirms existing orders but recognises the boundary ministry of deacons in some pastoral settings.

From our consultations and discussions it seems to us that, without undermining the orders of ministry, in certain pastoral circumstances, particularly in a hospital chaplaincy context, a deacon might anoint the sick. Whilst anointing by a priest is, and remains, the norm, a situation where it might be appropriate for a deacon to anoint is where it would be an integral part of the ministry of the deacon to that person and it would either be difficult to wait for a priest to be found, or pastorally inappropriate to introduce a third person who does not know the history of the ongoing pastoral care provided by the deacon.

Questions have been raised in our consultations about the proclamatory ministry of deacons and the expectation that deacons should preach, since some people feel strongly that preaching is not a part of diaconal ministry. This approach is encapsulated in the dictum of St Francis, 'Preach the gospel, use words if necessary.' The Revd. Canon Robert Seifert[77] notes that most deacons only have the presbyteral prototype of preaching to emulate – which many deacons resist because they sense, intuitively, that it threatens the integrity of the diaconate. He also notes that in New Testament terms, preaching is a public proclamation of the gospel in the manner of a messenger or herald and that the Greek of the New Testament uses a wealth of words that have been translated into English as 'preach'. The limitations of English mean that many of the rich nuances of these Greek words are lost in the use of 'to preach' and we end up with a concept of proclaiming the gospel that is confined to preaching a sermon according to recognised rules of discourse. A further complication is our confusion of teaching and preaching, whereas in the New Testament these are distinct. Seifert traces the confusion through the Reformation where the reaction of English Puritans to the deplorable state of most preaching in parishes led them to elevate the sermon to the status of the medium for salvation. However Richard Hooker, who was sympathetic to the Puritans' complaints, did not agree with them that salvation was only effected through hearing sermons. Instead, he offered a much wider definition that described preaching as the proclamation of God's word by any public means, 'open publication of heavenly mysteries, is by an excellency termed Preaching.'[78]

There is a shift in emphasis from the ASB Ordinal to the trial liturgy for ordination as far as preaching is concerned. Whilst recognising that proclaiming the word of God can take many forms, we recommend that as part of their ministry of proclamation, all deacons are trained in the basics of preaching. This should include sermon preparation and delivery, since this can form a part (although not necessarily the majority) of the proclamatory and catechectical ministry of the deacon. In all cases, preaching should be complementary to the wider ministry of deacons, including caring, and may enhance it. For distinctive deacons who do not have a particular vocation to preaching week by week, the focus of their preaching training might be that of preaching at pastoral services. Where deacons have been pastorally involved with those attending the service their preaching can express in words their holistic diaconal ministry to these people. Equally, a deacon may be called upon to preach in a way that interprets to the church the needs of the world.

7. The Relationship of the Diaconate to Lay Ministries

7.1 The relationship of the diaconate to lay ministries

In this practical section of the report we look at the relationships envisaged in this diocese between those ordained to the diaconate and existing and well-established lay ministries. The theological relationship between ordained and lay ministry has already been discussed.

If we are to encourage vocations to the diaconate due attention must be given to the relationship of the deacon to the increasing number of people active in lay ministry. Authorised ministries include Readers, Lay Pastoral Assistants, Deaconesses, Accredited Lay Workers and the Church Army; in addition there is an increasing number of laity who lead non eucharistic worship, lead music and take up other identifiable roles within their parish team. The relationship can be fragile if lay people perceive the deacon as taking over or disempowering them. Continuing education and nurture amongst both clergy and laity are needed to ensure that the relationship is one of mutual strength and complementarity rather than competition and conflict. Anecdotal evidence gleaned from talking to those deacons already serving in the diocese shows that each situation has to be worked out sensitively within the parish, thereby asking the deacon to demonstrate exactly the skills that are sought in a diaconal vocation.

7.2 Deacons and Readers

Salisbury diocese has a large number of Readers, (approx 230) with about a quarter of that number, being aged over 70, having Permission to Officiate. Many of the Readers are of retirement age or have taken early retirement from their employment. The current trend for early retirement to Dorset and Wiltshire brought ten new Readers into the diocese in 2002. There is an encouraging number of potential Readers coming forward for selection and training, with eight beginning training in 2002. Readers are well affirmed in their work by the Board of Ministry with continuing education and support, and morale has been raised. Some Readers have later gone forward for ordination as OLMs and NSMs, but this is balanced by those coming forward for training as Reader. The now well-established OLM scheme in this Diocese has not affected Reader numbers.

The somewhat inadequate understanding of the relationship between Reader and deacon was less than helpful in the earlier General Synod debate. In encouraging the vocation to the diaconate, care will have to be taken to demonstrate that this ministry is complementary to that of the Readers and that Reader ministry is not being displaced or devalued. Vocational literature, teaching aids, training days and Sarum Link articles should all make this very clear, and clergy and training incumbents should have an increased awareness of the tensions that will inevitably arise if the two ministries are not understood. Those responsible for the Reader network will likewise have to educate Readers in the rightness of the calling of others to become deacons. With an increase profile for the vocation to the diaconate, it may be expected that there will be some Readers who will test their vocation to diaconal ministry, just as some currently test their vocation to the priesthood.

The promotion of Reader ministry in this diocese as a preaching and teaching ministry is clear, and initial training and Continuing Ministerial Education (CME) training focuses on this aspect of ministry. Parish pastoral ministry complements and enhances preaching and teaching and is the task of all the baptised, so Readers exercise a ministry which will of necessity include some pastoral work since effective preaching and teaching must be pastoral even when it is disturbing. In other words, it is part of a rainbow ministry which will always overlap, in part, with that of other people. Readers are increasingly exercising their ministry in the work place where theological understanding and the ability to express basic Christian truths makes their presence a vital one within areas that other ministry does not necessarily reach.

7.3 Deacons and Lay Pastoral Assistants

The training and commissioning of LPAs has been encouraging over the years, and there are now over 1000 registered LPAs in the diocese. The training scheme has been completely revised recently and has been adopted across the diocese to good effect. It provides a basic training in a range of pastoral work but does not equip the LPAs with a grounding in theological, biblical and liturgical studies, and neither does it train them to reflect theologically on their ministry.

Vocations to diaconal ministry may well flow from the ranks of our LPAs since a pastoral heart and pastoral gifts are part of the deacon's vocation. However, the ministry of the deacon is broader and deeper than that of the LPAs and most LPAs should be encouraged to continue their practical lay pastoral ministry and not confuse this with a diaconal vocation. Clergy may be aware of some LPAs whose ministry may be growing towards diaconal ministry and the guidelines we include later in this report will help with discerning where a specialized lay ministry is growing towards a diaconal vocation.

There is at least one parish in this diocese where the complementarity of the ministry of the deacon with that of several LPAs is evident and is a relationship we would wish to encourage in other parishes. The deacon not only oversees and facilitates the work of the LPAs, but is able to bring their ministry into the heart of the liturgical life of the church as well as to staff meetings. Handled well, with a clear understanding of the different ministries, the role of a deacon in relation to LPAs will be a vital growth point in ministry, providing a leadership focus and personal encouragement to lay people as they seek to serve God in their parishes.

7.4 Deacons and other lay ministries

At the present time this diocese has one Deaconess and one Licensed Lay Worker but no Church Army officers. There are seven Authorised Laypersons who have a licence to preach in connection with their position in sector ministry posts at Church House. There are also Youth, Children's and Community Workers licensed to minister in the diocese. Most appointed chaplains to schools, colleges, hospitals, almshouses and prisons are ordained clergy.

Parish deacons will of necessity be working in close contact with the increasing number of gifted and skilled lay people who readily take responsibility for leading non eucharistic worship (for example, all-age worship, family services and praise services), encouraging the music and singing in our churches, and working with children of all ages in Sunday Schools, youth groups, clubs and uniformed groups. Apart from being an important part of the liturgical ministry of the deacon, this can be a ministry among those on the edge of the church helping to bring them into the church, perhaps for a monthly parade service. The Board of Ministry, in encouraging the vocation, training and ordination of parish deacons, will need to work with the Board of Parish Development to establish support for incumbents and parishes in the working out of relationships and roles for the many different lay callings.

8. Current Practice

8.1 The Church of England

In December 1998 there were estimated to be 80 distinctive deacons in active ministry in the Church of England.[79] This contrasts with 13,104 priests at the same time (and with 900 deacons and 3400 priests in the Church of Sweden, 237 deacons and 1200 priests in the Church of Norway, and 1147 deacons or deaconesses in parishes and 200 in other church-related posts, and 1790 priests in the Evangelical Church of Finland).

A survey of 85 deacons in 1997-1998 produced an 81% response rate and thus gives fairly complete information.[80] 74% of the deacons who responded were female, 28% were ordained in 1987, the year when women were first ordained to the diaconate. They serve in 26 of the 43 Church of England dioceses (excluding the Diocese of Europe) with the largest concentrations in Portsmouth, Chichester and London. 15 of the 26 dioceses in the survey only had one deacon. 26% of the deacons had been deaconesses before ordination, but only 11% had been authorised lay workers or Readers. This last figure suggests that the fear that Deacons will replace Readers is unfounded in current practice.

51% of the respondents had held full time church appointments and 52% had held paid church appointments, but the figures are skewed by the fact that 26% of the respondents had been deaconesses for whom full time paid church appointments were available. Current appointment information suggests that full time paid church appointments are very rare, by 1999 there were only two deacons in Portsmouth and Chichester (the dioceses with most deacons) in full time stipendiary posts, although in the survey 33% reported that they worked in a full time non-stipendiary capacity. More than one in six of the survey respondents had had to accept non-stipendiary posts when they would have preferred a stipendiary post. Over one third of deacons in parishes devote more than 35 hours a week to their ministry. Deacons in sector ministries are paid by those who employ them but for Church of England purposes they are counted as non stipendiary.

In terms of what duties the deacons undertake, pastoral work accounts for 30% of their time, educational work 21%, liturgical work 20%, social action 14% and other duties 15%. Most worked on parish-based, short term projects although a few had developed work across a deanery or diocese. Few had national or international ecumenical involvement, although many were well-equipped for this and for a much wider scale of ministry than they seemed to have in practice. This suggests that, quite apart from the question of whether there should be more deacons, existing deacons are being under-used in the church, although 88% thought their duties were commensurate with their gifts.

The current situation (2002) in the Diocese of Portsmouth is that they have 20 distinctive deacons, all of whom are non-stipendiary and there are no plans to appoint stipendiary deacons. Some have paid part time chaplaincies in hospitals, but all are licensed to churches.[81]

8.2 The Diocese of Salisbury

There are, at present, six distinctive deacons in this diocese. Five are in parish ministry and one, whilst serving in a parish on Sundays, has a primary focus in a hospital where she is part of the chaplaincy team. One served as Bishop's Deacon until recently but is now in a parish. Four are OLMs and two are NSMs. Five trained within the diocese but not on recognised routes through the Southern Theological Education and Training Scheme (STETS) or the Ordained Local Ministry (OLM) scheme, instead each had an abbreviated training – a subject to which we will return later. In addition, there are three people who have completed two years of a three year training for the diaconate, two via STETS for non-stipendiary ministry and one via the OLM scheme.

8.3 Summary of consultations with deacons and deacons in training

These notes summarise interviews with the deacons and those in training in the Diocese of Salisbury in 2002. Most had gone forward to the selection process without specifically offering themselves to be deacons. It was through conversation with The Revd. Canon Stanley Royle (then Diocesan Director of Ordinands) or Bishop John Kirkham that the possibility of being ordained to the permanent diaconate emerged. At least two of them would have been priested had this been offered to them as a possibility, while the others always desired a supporting ministry and wish to remain as deacons. Two of the deacons see very little difference practically between Readers and deacons. One of the deacons had been a Reader before ordination and two had been LPAs.

All of the deacons in parish ministry have a liturgical role, though this varies from one parish to another. One deacon, for instance, is heavily involved in the Sunday School and so has less opportunity for deaconing at the Eucharist than the others. The deacon at Poole Hospital also has less opportunity for expressing her ministry liturgically. Pastorally, the deacons are involved in a variety of ways. Those in parishes are involved in baptism and wedding preparation. Most also take funerals regularly, and visit the sick. One deacon now acts as a facilitator for the monthly LPA meetings in the parish. There is some (though this is not universal) disquiet among the deacons that they are not allowed to conduct baptisms except in an emergency, especially since deacons are involved in baptism preparation. As far as preaching is concerned, there is a variety of practice. Some deacons preach regularly once a month or more often, others only rarely, perhaps once or twice a year.

The selection procedures for deacons came under some criticism. Part of this is due to a bad personal experience of the interviews, but some of the criticism was more general. One deacon felt that all clergy should be selected through the same process and advocated using the more locally based OLM selection procedure and abolishing ABM (now Ministry Division) selection conferences.[82] Another deacon had had a bad experience with the OLM interview, perhaps reflected in the fact that among the deacons there are some who were not recommended by the Selectors and others who resented not being able to 'go on' to the priesthood.

The training of deacons also came in for some heavy criticism. Most were of the opinion that what they had received was of good quality, but that there was not enough of it. The shortened training course put together for the three deacons ordained in 2000 was made up of parts of the OLM course, but it had not been fully developed at the time.

The CME on offer is the same as that for all other clergy in years 1– 4. Much of it is commended, but there are some parts of CME which were thought to be irrelevant to deacons, and the handling of the change from year 1 to year 2 needs to be sensitive as most clergy go on to be priested at that point. One deacon said that sometimes the permanent deacons feel "invisible" in CME.

The attitudes of the deacons varied considerably. There is still some resentment from those who would have preferred to be subsequently ordained to the priesthood, while those who are happy to remain deacons seemed to have a far more positive attitude to the whole process.

9. The Fostering of Diaconal Vocations

9.1 How can we foster vocations to the distinctive diaconate?

If the diocese is to take seriously the ministry of the deacon, vocations nurturing, testing and selection processes must ensure that people have a clear vocation to this particular ministry. The diaconate should be understood as a vocation in its own right and should neither be seen as a second class vocation for those who will not 'make it' as a priest nor a 'reward' for faithful lay ministry. Both approaches diminish the distinctive vocation of the deacon, undermine the church's threefold order of ministry and devalue lay ministry. To that end, much needs to be done in the parishes to raise awareness of the diaconal ministry, which regrettably is still seen in some quarters as a new and additional layer of ministry that is 'not quite a priest', further diminishes the ministry of the laity and threatens the ministry of Readers.

There is a need in the parishes for education about ministry in general, including the ecclesiological perspectives and the interweaving of liturgy and ministry. This would lay the groundwork not only to help to overcome the lack of understanding about the diaconate, but also to help people live into their baptismal vocation and provide a firm basis for the nurture of vocations to all forms of ministry. This recommendation could be referred to the Board of Parish Development as well as to the Vocations Group.

Many of the clergy are so used to the diaconate as a transitional year that they have little appreciation of the distinctive ministry of deacons. Opportunities therefore should be taken to increase the clergy's theological and ecclesiological understanding of diaconal ministry. In our discussions with deacons and those in training it has been evident that where they and their incumbents have a clear sense of their vocation to the diaconate they also have a clearer understanding of the threefold order of ministry. However, those for whom the diaconate is a 'second choice' of vocation tend to have much less clear understandings of the distinctive vocation of a deacon, and both they and their parish struggle to come to terms with what they cannot do, because they are not priests, rather than what they are called to as deacons.

If parishes can become excited and enthused about what the richness of diaconal ministry will enable all them to do, perhaps through a roadshow approach to excite and inform them, there is greater scope for a variety of patterns collaborative ministry in each church. The Vocations Group has indicated that a leaflet on 'Who'd be a Deacon?' will be prepared, to complement those on being a Priest, a Reader and a Lay Pastoral Assistant. A further leaflet about the varieties of ministry, not just these four already listed, would be helpful in setting a wider canvas for people and parishes considering vocations. This should include a brief theological and ecclesiological explanation of ministry in the diocese. However, the best advertisements for the diaconal ministry are deacons themselves. The diocese should find ways to use its deacons and their parishes to foster interest in the diaconate in other parishes. The Vocations Group should be encouraged to include deacons in their Vocations Days.

A note may be helpful about what to call the deacons whose vocations we encourage. Reports vary in using 'Permanent Deacon', 'Distinctive Deacon' or just 'Deacon' (on the basis that those to be priested are 'Transitional Deacons'). We have tended to opt for 'Distinctive Deacon' because 'Transitional Deacon' implies that priests leave their diaconate behind once priested, whilst 'Permanent Deacon' also suggests that others are impermanent deacons. In the Diocese of Portsmouth, which has been at the forefront of renewing the diaconate, the deacons prefer to describe themselves as 'Distinctive Deacons' because a few of them have, after several years as deacons, tested a vocation to the priesthood that has gradually grown out of their diaconal ministry. They feel that 'Permanent Deacon' does not recognise that a different vocation may develop later, whereas 'Distinctive Deacon' both affirms their vocation and allows for the few cases where something new emerges.

Recommendation 1: *The Diocese of Salisbury will foster vocations to the distinctive diaconate as part of the threefold order of ministry in the Church. In so doing, the Diocese will look for a clear vocation to the diaconate and not a failed vocation to another ministry.*

Recommendation 2: *The threefold order of ministry should be reflected in a clear understanding of the ministry of deacons. To this end, the diocese should work to increase understanding of the diaconate among clergy and laity and consideration* *should be given to using the Sarum Link to facilitate this. Appropriate training resources for the parishes that set ministry in its theological and ecclesiological contexts should be made available. As part of this, vocations leaflets on 'Who'd be a Deacon?' and on varieties of ministry should be produced. Parishes should be enthused about the richness of ministry and helped to encourage and identify diaconal ministries among their members.*

Recommendation 3: *Understanding of the diaconate should be increased among clergy (in particular training incumbents) and Readers. To this end consideration should be given to using the resources of, the CME programme and the Southern Regional Institute (SRI).*

9.2 Are we looking for stipendiary or non stipendiary Deacons?

In the Scandinavian churches most deacons are stipendiary clergy. There are historical reasons for this, arising from the dominant emphasis of their ministry in the social, nursing and educational professions and the fact that for the most part the church has provided these services on behalf of the state. In recognition of this, the state and the local authorities either employ the deacons directly or contribute funding for their ministry. Concomitantly, the liturgical role of the deacon in these churches is frequently minimal or non-existent. This is a very different context to our own in this country.

'For such a time as this' refers to both stipendiary and non stipendiary deacons and recommends that stipendiary distinctive deacons should be placed on the same scale of stipend as other assistant clergy.[83] This principle of parity for those clergy who are stipendiary was misinterpreted in the General Synod debate to mean that all distinctive deacons will be stipendiary. The report itself provides no foundation for this assumption.

Just as, at present, there are both stipendiary and non stipendiary priests as well as OLM priests, we envisage that there will be stipendiary, non stipendiary and OLM deacons. At present nearly all stipendiary deacons are subsequently ordained priest and exercise their diaconal ministry at the same time as their priestly ministry. The existing pattern of ministry in this diocese places emphasis on collaborative teams which include stipendiary and non stipendiary clergy and lay people. This helps to avoid a situation where the diaconal ministry of the church is perceived to be the preserve of stipendiary clergy. As with the other ministries, there is scope in many parishes for more than one deacon. Indeed, to have a group of deacons working together would model something very significant that is lost when ministry is seen as an individual vocation.

Since the deacon's ministry embraces boundaries between the church and the world in which deacons are deeply involved on a daily basis, there will be deacons who understand their calling to be Ministers in Secular Employment (MSE). At present the diocese has one deacon whose focus of ministry is the hospital. This was also the context in which her diaconal vocation was identified and nurtured. We anticipate that there could be further diaconal vocations focused on sector ministries and recommend that they be encouraged. In such cases, clear links with a parish are essential, but there should be early discussions to ensure that all concerned understand the two threads of diaconal ministry involved.

Where there is a vocation to stipendiary ministry, we recommend that the deacon is not automatically included as part of the Clergy Allocation under the Sheffield formula, but that alternative financial resources be explored which may reflect the focus of their ministry. For example, a deacon in Slough who works with the disadvantaged in the community is largely financed by the local authority. Another scenario could be a parish youth worker who is ordained deacon but is paid as a youth worker. However, there will be situations where it is appropriate for the deacon to be stipendiary and included in the Sheffield numbers. We recognise that there may be some opposition to this among people whose understanding of stipendiary ministry is limited to that of priests and who perceive that they are being denied a priest because of the deacon. Rather than deny the diaconal vocation, what is needed in such circumstances is education to raise awareness of the depth and texture of the church's ministry: the solution in this case might be to have a stipendiary deacon and a Non-Stipendiary Minister (NSM) or OLM priest on the ministry team.

Although we are assuming that, in the immediate future, most deacons will continue to be NSMs, OLMs or MSEs, it should be noted that this does not necessarily equate with matters of deployability. Later we will raise the possibility of deacons offering their ministry within the deanery where this is appropriate.

Recommendation 4: *In the Diocese of Salisbury, diaconal ministry may include stipendiary ministry, NSM, OLM and MSE. Diaconal ministry may be focused on a chaplaincy, but in such circumstances the deacon should also be rooted in a local church. Where there is a vocation to stipendiary diaconal ministry, the possibility of alternative funding that reflects the particular nature of the diaconal ministry concerned should be explored, but the absence of such funding should not be determinative of whether or not the diaconal ministry is affirmed.*

9.3 The selection of deacons

The reception given to 'For such a time as this' indicates the lack of clarity in the Church of England on the ministry of the deacon. Therefore, to ensure that selectors are fully aware of the encouragement of diaconal ministry in this diocese, when candidates are sent to Selection Conference the diocesan understanding of the ministry of deacons should be made clear along with guidance on what we are looking for in our deacons.

Since concern has been expressed that many distinctive deacons transfer to the priesthood after a few years, we consulted the Diocese of Portsmouth to ascertain the situation there. According to their Director of NSM Ordinands, in the past, a few ordinands were channelled down the diaconal route even though they really felt a call to the priesthood and as a consequence they have subsequently sought transfer of category to priesthood. In such circumstances, if they trained at Chichester they completed a further year of training at STETS or if they trained at STETS they completed a programme of priestly formation. Last year four were ordained to the priesthood and this year there will be two, but after that the diocese does not anticipate many requests for transfer since the vocations testing procedures are clearer. This experience reaffirms the importance of clarity at selection about the nature of the vocation.

Recommendation 5: *When candidates are sent to Selection Conference, the Diocesan Director of Ordinands will provide the selectors with a clear statement of the diocesan understanding of the ministry of the deacon along with the sense of vocation and gifting the Diocese looks for in deacons.*

9.4 What do we look for in a deacon?

The ministry of the deacon is wide-ranging, 'For such a time as this' highlighted three strands to the ministerial profile – pastoral, liturgical and catechetical – and raised questions about a fourth, administration. These are addressed in chapter 7 of 'For such a time as this' which we append to this report. Without repeating everything in this chapter, we highlight some of its key principles that have shaped our thinking.

'For such a time as this' states that, although the deacon has a distinctive ministry, this does not include ultimate responsibility for the cure of souls, but assistance to those who do.[84] It notes that the collegial nature of this collaboration is not reflected in the Ordinal in the Alternative Service Book 1980 (ASB) and neither is the deacon's relationship to the bishop made explicit. The ASB also fails to draw attention to the deacon's involvement in social issues of justice and community building, and his or her ministry of bringing these to the heart of the church's life through the liturgy. Positively, deacons are agents of the ministry of Christ himself with a special role to make connections and build bridges between the distinctive life, the koinonia, of the Body of Christ and the needs of the world. They help to build up the visibility of the church in the local community and with civil society through their ministry as ordained representative ministers. The calling of the deacon is to focus, encourage and help co-ordinate the *diakonia* (the divine commission) of the whole church within the mission of God in the world. Deacons can help the church to connect, and are a major missing link in the church's ministry and mission. It is important that the distinctive voice of the diaconate is heard in the conciliar life of the church and in ecumenical contexts. The comment in the report about the cure of souls raised for the Working Party the distinction between the cure of souls as responsibility, which lies with the priest, and the cure of souls as pastoral process in which the deacon shares. This highlights the need for diaconal training in pastoral care and in collaborative ministry.

Earlier in this report (Section 2.5) we referred to the Nordic emphasis on deacons having prior professional qualifications in the social, educational or nursing professions. We noted the different understanding of diaconal ministry in these churches from that in the Church of England. We also discussed the challenges to the Church of England from the recent and anticipated changes in welfare provision. We believe that the Church of England should be ready to learn from the Nordic churches and the other Reformation churches where the diaconate is primarily about service, without adopting their ecclesiology in relation to the diaconate. If the Church of England is to respond to the growing need for services that were previously provided by the Welfare State, there is a need to encourage diaconal vocations among people who bring some experience (whether or not this is expressed in a professional qualification) in the caring fields. This should not be a pre-requisite for diaconal ministry, but a potential source of diaconal vocations that is explored actively. Neither should a professional qualification in an appropriate field be considered a passport to ordination, but the wider diaconal vocation should be tested since this includes the exemplification of the interdependence of worship and service.

As an alternative to the description of the ministry of the deacon in 'For such a time as this', the Working Party proposes an alternative way of describing the ministry of the deacon focused not so much on its content as on where it takes place. In our discussions, we highlighted the following strands of diaconal ministry:

The deacon in the church:

- has a non-presidential, representative ministry, representing Christ's own diaconal ministry;

- is the eyes and ears of the Bishop and, particularly in parishes which are part of teams or benefices, of the Team Rector;

- participates in the liturgy,

- proclaims the word of God and preaches where this is necessary or pastorally appropriate, recognising that some but not all deacons are gifted in preaching, and that in this diocese there is a strong Reader ministry;

- as a person with a ministry that is pastoral, catechetical and liturgical, helps to make connections for the children between their age-appropriate teaching and their inclusion in the liturgical life of the church;

- shares the preparation of people for pastoral or liturgical rites, including baptism, confirmation and marriage, and accompanies those concerned when they come to the church, sharing in the liturgy as appropriate, perhaps presenting them, or baptising them;

- has a prophetic role in drawing the church's attention to peace and justice issues that the church is overlooking;

- shares in the pastoral care of those who look to the church and facilitates the ministry of Lay Pastoral Assistants, by co-ordinating and supporting their work. In so doing they exemplify the role of the clergy in facilitating the ministry of others and have a representative role that is beyond the functional work of Lay Pastoral Assistants.

- brings and interprets the needs of the world to the church's worship and pastoral care;

- helps to order the church in administration, perhaps at a deanery rather than just a parochial level.

The deacon in the world:

- is equipped to see Christ in the midst of the life of the world, whether locally or internationally;

- has a prophetic role in the world where need or injustice exist;

- brings the church's ministry of peace and justice to the world, either directly or by facilitating the ministry of others in the church;

- brings the pastoral ministry of the church to people in need, seeking out the lonely, the forgotten, the marginalised, the sick, those in trouble;

- makes the invisible ministry of the church visible;

- is the eyes and ears of the church in the local area.

The deacon on the boundary:

- is at the door of the church to greet people, particularly those encountered in ministry in the local area, helping them to cross the threshold into worship;

- is in the prophet's place on the edges and boundaries of society;

- is a two-way go-between or agent between church and world, straddling the boundary and helping others to cross it;

- brings the needs of the world over the boundary into church, and interprets them in intercession;

- sends people out from worship into the world, in peace and for service;

- is a catalyst for Christian discipleship in the mission space between worship and the world.

Given this vocation, what kind of person might be called to diaconal ministry? We have identified the following attitudes, qualities and giftings, either developed or in embryo, that might be looked for in a person considering a vocation to diaconal ministry:

- the support of the local church, and perhaps wider community, for their vocation;

- a strong sense of vocation to the ministry of the deacon, not a failed or thwarted sense of vocation somewhere else;

- a sense of a life-calling from God, not a potentially passing desire to engage in the church's ministry;

- the ability and willingness to work in a team;

- leadership gifts that reflect a willingness to be a leader who assists rather than always takes the lead, and does not unsettle or unseat others who have either long term or short term responsibilities;

- a person who is capable of being a public representative person for the church, who is competent and comfortable in the public eye, whether in liturgy or the life of the world;

- engagement with hidden ministry, a responsible behind the scenes person, able to be hidden, to get on with things out of the limelight, to oil the wheels;

- an attitude that reflects a vocation to be a servant without being a doormat;

- sensitivity, expressed in an ability to listen and appropriate body language that welcomes others whilst respecting their space;

- comfort occupying space on the boundaries, a liminal person who is at ease alongside people on the edges of the church and of society yet who is also secure and centred for themselves;

- an outgoing, risk-taking, world-oriented perspective;

- evidence of engagement with and in the local community, and awareness of what is happening in the wider world;

- evidence of a life of service within and outside the Christian community;

- evidence of ability to relate to people of different ages and social contexts;

- an instinctive ability to get alongside people and speak their language;

- pastoral skills that point to an ability to care for others appropriately;

- communication skills that enable the person to preach the gospel in deed and in word;

- teaching gifts, expressed in various and appropriate ways;

- liturgical sensitivity and presence that enables others to worship, brings the needs of the world into worship and interprets them for the Christian community;

- a rooted Christian spirituality, grounded in a life of prayer and immersion in God's word, attentive to God's presence in the world in its majesty and its misery;

- a quality of mind that reflects a thirst to know more of God and an ability to interpret what is known for others;

- creativity and imagination coupled with stability and common sense;

- organisational gifts that equip and free others to do their work well;

- a passion for God and for life, and a refusal to allow stagnation to set in, personally or in the church.

Not everyone is gifted in all these ways, but the deacon's attitudes should point to a way of life in which many of these gifts are displayed already and others might grow.

Recommendation 6: *In the vocations testing and selection processes for deacons, the Diocese of Salisbury will look for a comfortable 'fit' with the ministerial profile and personal giftings listed in section 9.4 of this report and in chapter 7 of For such a time as this.*

10. The Initial Training of Deacons

10.1 Training for ministry in the Diocese of Salisbury

At present, non-stipendiary deacons are trained at STETS where they train alongside people preparing for stipendiary or non stipendiary ministry or authorised lay ministry in the Church of England, the Methodist Church and the United Reformed Church. Ordained Local Ministry deacons train on the Ordained Local Ministry Scheme alongside Readers, they also share some study days with STETS students. A group of three deacons trained together via the OLM route using some of the pilot scheme course materials but with an abbreviated training, and two other deacons have followed personalised and truncated training that was intended to build on previous Reader training.

Those deacons who have trained or are at present training alongside people training for other ministry express the value of this and do not want to be trained separately. There is a strong message that they want the full three years, they express the view that anything less than this does not equip them adequately. The three deacons who trained together on a shortened programme express frustration that their training was inadequate because it was rushed and did not cover all that they now realise they need to know. This is borne out by their need to look (not always successfully) to CME to fill gaps in their knowledge or experience that their peers in CME filled in initial training. There are similar serious concerns about the inadequacy of training for those who had personalised abbreviated training, which in practice meant doing a few modules from the overall training programme. From the perspective of the Board of Ministry staff, such shortened and tailor-made training is both inadequate for the student, especially in the formational aspects and the lack of a peer group at residentials and tutorials, and inordinately time consuming for the staff. It is the deacons who had shortened training who struggle most with a clear sense of a diaconal vocation as distinct from other vocations. This points to the benefits of three years as a time of transition and growing into the new vocational identity, quite apart from the educational need for three years. A true vocation need not be rushed.

The modules used in initial training at STETS and OLM provide a basic educational grounding that equips people for ordained or lay ministry. Some involve contextual studies which help students to ground their academic learning in the local area, these are of particular value to deacons (whether transitional or distinctive deacons). The emphasis of the STETS course is ministry and mission, and examination of the academic modules indicates that there is no need for any amendments in order to meet specific needs of distinctive deacons. The formational aspects of training are focused towards ordained ministry and since all will be ordained deacon at the end of their studies it is appropriate that there should be a diaconal strand to this formation work. As a result of consultations, STETS staff are willing to look again at the formational modules and to insert further diaconal formation material. Similarly, the OLM staff will ensure that the formational module that supplements STETS training for OLMs will include appropriate diaconal material. Whilst those who anticipate ordination to the priesthood at a later date will undoubtedly also be beginning to think of priestly formation, we recommend that this should not be a major emphasis in initial training but be addressed more specifically in CME.

It could be possible for a stipendiary deacon to train at a full time college. However, given the availability of good training resources at STETS and the OLM scheme, and the general emphasis on priestly ministry at the full time colleges, the disadvantages of a deacon doing all their training *via* a full time college course outweigh any benefits. However, an alternative of spending a month at a full time college could provide a valuable perspective for some students training on courses or schemes. Two STETS students have already done this and STETS are willing to explore other possibilities in response to the needs of individual students.

Bishop Otter College at Chichester provides a diaconal formation programme as a component of its Diploma in Theology and Ministry. There are ongoing discussions between STETS and Bishop Otter about the opportunities for co-operation between the two courses. There may be scope for Salisbury deacons to take advantage of the resources available through Bishop Otter and the most appropriate way to facilitate this is through the links that STETS and Bishop Otter are building up. This could apply equally to deacons training for OLM, given that they use STETS modules as part of their training. We note that the Diocese of Portsmouth used the Bishop Otter course in the past for its deacons but now trains them through STETS.

All students undertake a placement during training, both STETS students and OLM students do this in a context that is different to their own. OLMs have to do their main placement in a church but also complete a short attachment in a sector ministry. STETS students have a choice of church or other context for their placement and many choose a sector placement. For some STETS students who are preparing for ministry as a distinctive deacon, it may be appropriate to recommend that they do their placement in a sector ministry; this does not require any alteration to the course materials, only informed thinking and decision making when the placement is set up.

Specifically in relation to preaching, we discussed earlier in the report (6.7) that deacons should proclaim the gospel in word and deed, in ways appropriate to the situations in which they are called to minister. Since this may on occasions include preaching, all deacons should be trained to preach although this may be focused on preaching at (for example) pastoral services or children's services, depending upon the particular focus of the deacon's ministry.

Recommendation 7: *All deacons will undertake a three year training via STETS or the OLM scheme. Where appropriate, this may include a short time at a full time college or Bishop Otter College. Where a student has prior experience, for example Reader training, allowance for this should be made not by abbreviating their training for ordained ministry but by consideration of their suitability for Accredited Prior Learning which would permit them to begin their studies at the diploma rather than certificate level. The fact of a diaconal vocation should be borne in mind when the placement location is being considered.*

Recommendation 8: *The proclamatory and catechectical ministry of deacons should be neither defined as, nor exclusive of, preaching. Deacons should model a proclamation of the gospel in word and deed that embodies their particular gifts and abilities, and is appropriate to the situations in which they are called to minister. Therefore, whilst all deacons should be trained to preach, this may be expressed in preaching primarily at pastoral services.*

10.2 Other approaches to training

We have looked at the training programme that the Diocese of Pittsburgh, USA, has developed for its substantial number of distinctive deacons. Although the method of delivery (evening classes) is different to that offered to our deacons, the content is basically the same and it lasts for three years. The key differences are that they provide an introduction to the diaconate and a practical course in pastoral care for deacons which is supplemented by a three month placement that centres on practical application of learning. The Diocese of Los Angeles has a School for Deacons, based at the Church Divinity School of the Pacific, which combines taught weekend courses with home study and leads to a bachelor's degree in Theological Studies. The academic studies are supplemented by spiritual formation and liturgical practice.

We have also looked at the course outline for the Roman Catholic Diocese of Clifton where a four year training course has some common elements with STETS/OLM, but with more emphasis on moral theology, ecclesiology, canon law, the sacraments and the church and less on contextual ministry and theology. The academic learning is supplemented by modules on spiritual development and pastoral development.

The Methodist Church advises training institutes that,

> Deacons require just as rigorous, wider ranging and deep grounding in theology as presbyters. Indeed, it could be argued that the innovative, community-based nature of their appointments requires even greater theological knowledge and skills of reflection and interpretation. ... It is important that student deacons train with presbyteral colleagues, it is also necessary for them to have opportunities for gathering with other diaconal students and for learning from experienced deacons.'[85]

Whilst the details of the training are left to the individual training institution, the basic syllabus for Methodist diaconal formation includes: the history and theology of the diaconate in the context of the three orders of ministry and relationship to the ministry of the whole people of God; the history, theology and characteristics of the Methodist Diaconal Order; images and symbols of the diaconate/diaconal ministry; theology and spirituality and contemporary issues in church, society and the ecumenical scene.

In response to the other models of training, we note that the practical training for our deacons is delivered in the parish, guided by the training agreements that all students have during training and in CME. We address questions of CME for deacons later in this report, but note here that there should be continuity between initial training and CME for all people. This is a matter for ongoing discussion between those responsible for initial training and CME. For deacons, the training agreements should reflect the particular vocation of the student.

We note the emphasis on history and theology of the diaconate in some of these other training courses. In our discussions about training in this diocese, we also noted the need for all students, whether for Ordained or Reader ministry, to understand how the ministry to which they are called fits in with other ministries. Recommendation 10, below, will also apply to Lay Pastoral Assistants since they should understand the relationship of their ministry to others, in particular to that of deacons.

Recommendation 9: *All students in initial training should receive basic ministry training in their parish, guided by their training agreement. This should thread seamlessly into the CME training agreement. Attention should be given to ensure that training agreements reflect the particular needs of distinctive deacons whose ministry may be focused slightly differently from transitional deacons.*

Recommendation 10: *Training for all authorised ministries in the Diocese of Salisbury should include teaching about the ecclesiology and theology of ministry in the Anglican church in order to enable the student to understand the ministry to which they are called in its ecclesiological and collaborative contexts.*

10.3 Diaconal formation

Formation for deacons begins before selection, in that candidates should demonstrate a vocation to this ministry. During initial training, students training at both STETS and as OLMs are guided in their ministerial formation by Developing Ministry Modules. These provide a framework for the student's growth both generally as a Christian and specifically towards ordained ministry within the Anglican Church. This formation takes place in many ways, including reading, prayer, reflective practice and practical experience.

Ninni Smedberg, a deacon in the Church of Sweden, draws attention to the particular strands of a spirituality for the deacon which reflects their calling.[86] She begins from the Swedish ordination liturgy which instructs deacons 'Meet people tenderly and with respect. Together with them, seek the way God wills, and let it be your endeavour to let faith, doctrine and life become one.' This is expressed in a question to the deacon, 'Will you so live among people that you bear witness to the love of God and to the mystery of reconciliation?' She points out that deacons are often so immersed in practical work that they do not find the time or inclination to talk about spirituality, and that often the deacon's personal spirituality determines the diaconal identity rather than the deacon's identity forming the spirituality.

The concerns raised by Smedberg appear to be a particular issue in some of the Scandinavian churches where the starting point of much diaconal ministry is professional qualification coupled with a faith focused on personal piety, to which formation in a local church is tacked on much later. It may not be such an issue in the Church of England but should in any case be addressed by the teaching on Anglican theology of ministry and spirituality. Like all clergy, deacons should engage in theological reflection on their ministry not only on their own but also with their incumbent and ministry team. Other opportunities may arise with their diaconal colleagues at their deacons' meetings.

From the Orthodox tradition comes the question whether, since the deacon perhaps more than any other order is called directly to minister to spiritually hungry people, candidates themselves require more spiritual preparation than is typically expected of clergy.[87] The thinking here is that deacons find themselves engaging with people on the margins of society and the church, thus with a large element of evangelism, witness and engagement with social issues, whereas priests are more concerned with spiritual growth and nurture. If the answer to the question is 'yes' then particular attention needs to be given to diaconal spiritual formation both in initial training and in CME.

This would benefit transitional deacons as well as distinctive deacons, and since the former are the potential training incumbents of the future it should help in the long term to increase clergy awareness of the distinctive vocation of the deacon.

11. Continuing Ministerial Education

11.1 CME 1–4 and the Distinctive Diaconate

The Diocesan CME 1–4 programme is designed to supplement the ministerial formation and development being carried out within the parochial and sector ministry. The importance of the process of ministerial formation cannot be underestimated during initial training and CME. Much of this is the responsibility of the training incumbent, but the CME 1–4 programme should serve to assist this formation process, and should allow for the formation both of deacons who will go on to become priests and those who remain as distinctive deacons. The ministerial training specification guides and encourages ministerial experience in the parish that is appropriate to the order and type of ministry concerned.

At present CME 1–4 is a programme that serves all the newly ordained, stipendiary, NSM and OLM, priests and deacons. From September 2002, Readers also share the first three years of the programme. It is important that priests, deacons and Readers understand the ministry of the others as well as growing into their own particular vocation, and that all learn ways in which to minister collaboratively. We note, though, that some of the negative comments about CME 1–4 from the existing distinctive deacons have arisen because they have felt, rightly or wrongly, that parts of the CME programme were not applicable to them. This may arise from an overly-functional view of CME. The CME staff point to the emphasis in the CME handbook on group sharing, support and development, and that CME should be a vehicle for group and personal formation rather than a provider of specific competencies. We recognise that there is a need for particular sensitivity, especially at the end of the first year of CME when many deacons will be preparing for ordination as priests while some of the CME year group will remain as deacons, and the need for visiting speakers not to assume that all the ordained people present are or will be priests.

Meetings of the group of distinctive deacons within the diocese already take place on a regular basis, which help to provide mutual support and encouragement, as well as a sharing of good practice between deacons. These meetings might also be used to address any additional CME needs that are specific to deacons.

Recommendation 11: *CME 1–4 should continue to be integrated and should be planned with sensitivity to the needs of all ministries represented. The reasons for the integrated philosophy of CME should be made clear to all participants.*

11.2 CME for training incumbents and other parish clergy

We have already noted that there remains a widespread lack of awareness among clergy about the value of the diaconate. There are still a number of clergy who believe that a curate is not much use to them until they are ordained to the priesthood. The Working Party has not conducted a comprehensive survey, but there is sufficient anecdotal evidence to suggest that clergy as well as lay people are largely unaware of the benefits of diaconal ministry. In advocating an enhanced role for the permanent diaconate, it is particularly important that training incumbents see the possibilities that the diaconate offers to enrich parish ministry, rather than regretting the priestly ministry that their curate is not providing. In the fostering of vocations to the distinctive diaconate, it is vital that all clergy and lay people are made aware of benefits of diaconal ministry.

To this end, as well as providing more frequent communication about the diaconate through *Sarum Link* and vocations material, there should be provision in the regular CME programme for clergy to learn more about the role of diaconal ministry in a parish or sector ministry setting. Such provision should be strongly recommended for any existing or potential training incumbents. Additionally, training incumbents of permanent deacons should be aware of their special needs when drawing up a training contract during the CME 1–4 programme. This should be addressed at the beginning of the deacon's ministry. Recommendation 3 at the end of section 9.1 addresses the CME needs of parish clergy.

12. Ongoing Support for Deacons

12.1 The Deacons Group

There is now a Deacons' Group within the diocese. Until recently it has comprised those who have been ordained, but now it also includes those in training for the distinctive diaconate. The existing members of the group value the opportunity to meet together as deacons, and the group should be encouraged to continue. If we learn from the Methodists of the value of mutual support for diaconal ministry, this deacons' group could be of immense importance in sustaining the deacons in their ministry on the margins. Some ongoing formational work for deacons can undoubtedly take place through sharing of resources and experiences in this group. In the light of our exploration of the ecumenical perspectives on the diaconate, the group may want to consider occasional meetings with local deacons from other denominations for mutual sharing and enrichment. We are also aware of The Revd. Roy Overthrow's visit to the Diocese of Evreux, and the benefit that flowed from that, and recommend that the Deacons' group explore the opportunities for similar visits in the future.

Recommendation 12: *The Deacons' Group should be encouraged to continue its development as a context for the nurture of diaconal ministry. The possibility of meetings with deacons in other denominations should be explored either through occasional local meetings or longer visits and exchanges.*

12.2 The relationship of Bishop and Deacons

We noted earlier in the report (Section 2.4) the particular relationship between the bishop and deacons which has always been present in the church, albeit more obviously at some times than others. Very often this relationship is more talked about than apparent in practice, and we feel that there could be immense benefits if attention were given to nurturing and making visible this relationship. Nurturing the relationship would be an encouragement to the deacons and would allow mutual exploration of ways that the deacons can assist the bishop. Making the relationship visible, particularly (but not exclusively) in the liturgy, and particularly on occasions when all the clergy are present (for example, the Chrism Eucharist, Clergy Conference and Synod) would restore a missing link in the pattern of ministry in the church. It would also play a part in the educational work that needs to be done if the ministry of the deacon is to be understood. The Deacons' Group can provide a ready made context for strengthening the relationship and we recommend that bishop and deacons meet at least once a year, using this group or other opportunities to strengthen and make visible their particular relationship.

Recommendation 13: *The relationship between the bishop and deacons should be nurtured and made visible in the ministry of the church. In order to facilitate this, they should meet together at least once a year to explore ways of enabling one another's ministry. The opportunities presented by the Deacons' Group should be taken where appropriate.*

13. Financial Implications

The financial implications of a renewed distinctive diaconate fall into three main categories: vocations testing and selection, initial and ongoing training, and ministry costs.

The work of the Vocations Advisor and the Vocations Group already covers what is needed to identify and test vocations to ordained ministry in the diocese. The diocese would bear the cost of additional places at OLM Selection Conferences, a figure cannot be included since this varies depending upon the venue.

Training costs are met by Ministry Division for stipendiary and non-stipendiary ministry and, since we recommend that all training is via STETS or the OLM scheme, the diocese will not have to meet the costs of grants to families of those in full time training. Training costs for OLMs are divided between the diocese, the parishes, Ministry Division and the student. Costs per student at present are: STETS fees (£900), book and vestments grant (£600) residentials and study days (£900) tutors (£150) and modules (£400). This total of £2950 is effectively covered by the grant for OLMs from Ministry Division (currently £720 pa) and the Parish contributions (£250 p.a.), leaving a cost to the diocese of £40 per student over the three years. The diocese also bears the cost of stipends and housing for staff involved in training OLMs. If the combined OLM group grows above 25 (we have 22 students this year) then it is likely at the next inspection of the OLM scheme we will be required to appoint additional staff. However, as 11 of the current students will finish their training this summer, this eventuality is unlikely arise in the immediate future unless the total number of new OLM vocations increases considerably. Parishes pay travel costs and an annual fee of £250 which effectively covers course materials for the parish group. The cost for each additional student would therefore be about £40 to the diocese and £750 plus travel costs to the parish over the three years.

Once ordained, the deacon would participate in the CME programme with all other clergy which is provided by the diocese. The number of CME year group tutors is responsive to the size of the year group; tutors are not paid so the only additional costs would be travel and expenses for any additional tutors that are needed. The parish would pay expenses for the deacon as for all other clergy. If the deacon were included in the Sheffield numbers, there would be the costs of a stipend and housing.

The Deacons' Group has requested help with reimbursing the expenses of any visiting speaker they invite to their meetings and the costs of administration of the group. The Board of Ministry budget includes small amounts of financial support to other similar groups (NSM Group, Women's Ministry, Health and Healing, Deliverance) and it would be appropriate to add the Deacons' Group with effect from the 2004 budget, using Trust income for any expenses incurred in 2003. A figure of £150 per year is suggested.

Recommendation 14: *A figure of £150 per annum should be included in the Board of Ministry budget from 2004 for the Deacons' Group. Any expenses up to £150 incurred during 2003 will be taken from Trust Funds.*

14. Deployment

We referred earlier to the fact that whether a deacon is stipendiary or not does not equate automatically to questions of deployability. At the moment all deacons in this diocese are parish based, although for one the main focus of ministry is the hospital and we hope that deacons might soon serve in other chaplaincies, for example in a prison, There are also questions about whether a deacon might be parish based yet serve a deanery, particularly if the deacon has particular gifts that are needed more widely. One example that has been suggested is that the ministry of a deacon with gifts of church administration might be valued not only by the Rural Dean but also some other parishes in the deanery.

Bishop Dr Walter Kasper,[88] writing from the Roman Catholic perspective, has suggested that whilst based in and tied to a definite parish, a deacon should be assigned to an area beyond that of the parish, to a town, deanery or region embracing a number of parishes. The deacon would use his home parish as a point of reference, but would perform diaconal tasks in other parishes and thus draw them together. His emphasis would be on the recruiting, training and support of volunteers in individual parishes. He should also be the natural point of contact with regional charities, associations and welfare services. The interesting suggestion here is not so much the work that the deacon would do, but the fact that this might serve a larger constituency than the parish in which the deacon is based.

Part of a deacon's role may be to go wherever they are needed. We make no specific recommendations about deployability of deacons, except to note that there is scope for creative use of diaconal ministry in the service of the church which we hope will be explored as new diaconal vocations emerge. This accords with the breadth and depth of ministry that falls to those who are on mission, messengers or ambassadors for God, icons of Christ.

15. Summary of Recommendations

In exploring the distinctive diaconate, we have become more convinced of the significance of the ministry of the deacon in the Church of England and excited by the possibilities for renewing this ministry in the church. We affirm the importance of the diaconate as an ordained ministry, part of the threefold order of ministry of the Church of England. Within the context of collaborative ministry that reflects and shares in the trinitarian life of God, the deacon is a sign to the church its own vocation to diaconal ministry in the service of Christ. The deacon does not do the work of others but encourages and enables the ministry of others, whether lay or ordained. The deacon's ministry is very much on the threshold, on the edges of church and society; the deacon is the church's representative person in a liminal ministry among those who would never cross the threshold of the church on their own. It is also a ministry within the church that keeps the needs of the world beyond the church door at the heart of the church's concern. The holistic nature of diaconal ministry holds together liturgical, catechetical and pastoral elements: it can never be just church social work, just leading worship, or just preaching or teaching, without losing its essential character.

It is important that we keep the ministry of the deacon visible rather than simply argue its details or its precise rationale. We recognise that we cannot derive a specific order of deacons from the New Testament although passages like Acts 6, where some people were set apart for a particular ministry, must be taken into account. The early church gives us examples of diaconal ministry, even if we do not recognise in them diaconal ministry in the precise form we know it today. Taken overall, we believe that there is sufficient evidence in the Christian tradition for diaconal ministry without having to seek justification for it in a precise model from the New Testament or the early church. The information we do have from the early centuries is complemented by more recent insights from other denominations which provide us with a rich tapestry of responses by the churches to the needs of the world, of which our own diaconate is but one. In the light of our denominational ecclesiology and understanding of ministry, we believe that the diaconate as we have inherited but re-examined it in the light of our twenty first century context is the right one for the Church of England at this time. In saying this about our own denomination, we hope that ecumenical contact among deacons will increase to everyone's mutual benefit.

Because of the demands of diaconal ministry, our deacons should be properly selected, well trained and formed, and given ongoing support. Complementing this, the vocation and ministry of deacons should be explained in the parishes so that all can understand the mutual relationships between the different lay and ordained ministries of the church – appreciating both the rainbow and the individual colours, the field of flowers and the particular flower.

We have met deacons or deacons in training for whom this is clearly the ministry to which they are called, and we rejoice at this 'fit' of person and vocation. We hope that this report will facilitate the vocation of other people to the diaconate so that the churches in the Diocese of Salisbury can fulfil their ministry better as our deacons shine a light on the servant ministry that is already embedded in our lives, exploding our awareness and understanding of Christ's diaconal ministry into a daily ministry.

Therefore, we recommend:

Encouraging the ministry of deacons

Recommendation 1: *The Diocese of Salisbury will foster vocations to the distinctive diaconate as part of the threefold order of ministry in the Church. In so doing, the Diocese will look for a clear vocation to the diaconate and not a failed vocation to another ministry.*

Recommendation 2: *The threefold order of ministry should be reflected in a clear understanding of the ministry of deacons. To this end, the diocese should work to increase understanding of the diaconate among clergy and laity and consideration should be given to using the resources of the Sarum Link to facilitate this. Appropriate training resources for the parishes that set ministry in its theological and ecclesiological contexts should be made available. As part of this, vocations leaflets on 'Who'd be a Deacon?' and on varieties of ministry should be produced. Parishes should be enthused about the richness of ministry and helped to encourage and identify diaconal ministries among their members.*

Recommendation 3: *Understanding of the diaconate should be increased among clergy (in particular training incumbents) and Readers. To this end consideration should be given to using the resources of the CME programme and the SRI.*

Recommendation 4: *In the Diocese of Salisbury, diaconal ministry may include stipendiary ministry, NSM, OLM and MSE. Diaconal ministry may be focused on a chaplaincy, but in such circumstances the deacon should also be rooted in a local church. Where there is a vocation to stipendiary diaconal ministry, the possibility of alternative funding that reflects the particular nature of the diaconal ministry concerned should be explored, but the absence of such funding should not be determinative of whether or not the diaconal ministry is affirmed.*

Selection of deacons

Recommendation 5: *When candidates are sent to Selection Conference, the Diocesan Director of Ordinands will provide the selectors with a clear statement of the diocesan understanding of the ministry of the deacon along with the sense of vocation and gifting the Diocese looks for in deacons.*

Recommendation 6: *In the vocations testing and selection processes for deacons, the Diocese of Salisbury will look for a comfortable 'fit' with the ministerial profile and personal giftings listed in section 9.4 of this report and in chapter 7 of For such a time as this.*

Initial and continuing training of deacons

Recommendation 7: *All deacons will undertake a three year training via STETS or the OLM scheme. Where appropriate, this may include a short time at a full time college or Bishop Otter College. Where a student has prior experience, for example Reader training, allowance for this should be made not by abbreviating their training for ordained ministry but by consideration of their suitability for Accredited Prior Learning which would permit them to begin their studies at the diploma rather than certificate level. The fact of a diaconal vocation should be borne in mind when the placement location is being considered.*

Recommendation 8: *The proclamatory and catechectical ministry of deacons should be niether defined as, nor exclusive of, preaching. Deacons should model a proclamation of the gospel in word and deed that embodies their particular gifts and abilities, and is appropriate to the situations in which they are called to minister.*

Therefore, whilst all deacons should be trained to preach, this may be expressed in preaching primarily at pastoral services.

Recommendation 9: *All students in initial training should receive basic ministry training in their parish, guided by their training agreement. This should thread seamlessly into the CME training agreement. Attention should be given to ensure that training agreements reflect the particular needs of distinctive deacons whose ministry may be focused slightly differently from transitional deacons.*

Recommendation 10: *Training for all authorised ministries in the Diocese of Salisbury should include teaching about the ecclesiology and theology of ministry in the Anglican church, in order to enable the student to understand the ministry to which they are called in its ecclesiological and collaborative contexts.*

Recommendation 11: *CME 1–4 should continue to be integrated and should be planned with sensitivity to the needs of all ministries represented. The reasons for the integrated philosophy of CME should be made clear to all participants.*

Support for diaconal ministry

Recommendation 12: *The Deacons' Group should be encouraged to continue its development as a context for the nurture of diaconal ministry. The possibility of meetings with deacons in other denominations should be explored either through occasional local meetings or longer visits and exchanges.*

Recommendation 13. *The relationship between the bishop and deacons should be nurtured and made visible in the ministry of the church. In order to facilitate this, they should meet together at least once a year to explore ways of enabling one another's ministry. The opportunities presented by the Deacons' Group should be taken where appropriate.*

Recommendation 14: *A figure of £150 per annum should be included in the Board of Ministry budget from 2004 for the Deacons' Group. Any expenses up to £150 incurred during 2003 will be taken from Trust Funds.*

The ministry of the deacon (Paragraph 9.4. See Recommendation 6)

The deacon in the church:

- *has a non-presidential, representative ministry, representing Christ's own diaconal ministry;*

- is the eyes and ears in the local area of the Bishop and, particularly in rural parishes, of the Team Rector;

- participates in the liturgy,

- proclaims the word of God and preaches where this is necessary or pastorally appropriate, recognising that some but not all deacons are gifted in preaching, and that in this diocese there is a strong Reader ministry;

- as a person with a ministry that is pastoral, catechetical and liturgical, helps to make connections for the children between their age-appropriate teaching and their inclusion in the liturgical life of the church;

- shares the preparation of people for pastoral or liturgical rites, including baptism, confirmation and marriage, and accompanies those concerned when they come to the church, sharing in the liturgy as appropriate, perhaps presenting them, or baptising them;

- has a prophetic role in drawing the church's attention to peace and justice issues that the church is overlooking;

- shares in the pastoral care of those who look to the church and facilitates the ministry of Lay Pastoral Assistants, by co-ordinating and supporting their work. In so doing they exemplify the role of the clergy in facilitating the ministry of others and have a representative role that is beyond the functional work of Lay Pastoral Assistants.

- brings and interprets the needs of the world to the church's worship and pastoral care;

- helps to order the church in administration, perhaps at a deanery rather than just a parochial level.

The deacon in the world:

- is equipped to see Christ in the midst of the life of the world, whether locally or internationally;

- has a prophetic role in the world where need or injustice exist;

- brings the church's ministry of peace and justice to the world, either directly or by facilitating the ministry of others in the church;

- brings the pastoral ministry of the church to people in need, seeking out the lonely, the forgotten, the marginalised, the sick, those in trouble;

- makes the invisible ministry of the church visible;

- is the eyes and ears of the church in the local area.

The deacon on the boundary:

- is at the door of the church to greet people, particularly those encountered in ministry in the local area, helping them to cross the threshold into worship;

- is in the prophet's place on the edges and boundaries of society;

- is a two-way go-between or agent between church and world, straddling the boundary and helping others to cross it;

- brings the needs of the world over the boundary into church, and interprets them in intercession;

- sends people out from worship into the world, in peace and for service;

- is a catalyst for Christian discipleship in the mission space between worship and the world.

Given this vocation, what kind of person might be called to diaconal ministry?(Paragraph 9.4)

- The following attitudes, qualities and giftings, either developed or in embryo, might be looked for in a person considering a vocation to diaconal ministry:

- the support of the local church, and perhaps wider community, for their vocation;

- a strong sense of vocation to the ministry of the deacon, not a failed or thwarted sense of vocation somewhere else;

- a sense of a life-calling from God, not a potentially passing desire to engage in the church's ministry;

- the ability and willingness to work in a team;

- leadership gifts that reflect a willingness to be a leader who assists rather than *always takes the lead, and does not unsettle or unseat others who have either long term or short term responsibilities;*

- *a person who is capable of being a public representative person for the church, who is competent and comfortable in the public eye, whether in liturgy or the life of the world;*

- *engagement with hidden ministry, a responsible behind the scenes person, able to be hidden, to get on with things out of the limelight, to oil the wheels;*

- *an attitude that reflects a vocation to be a servant without being a doormat;*

- *sensitivity, expressed in an ability to listen and appropriate body language that welcomes others whilst respecting their space;*

- *comfort occupying space on the boundaries, a liminal person who is at ease alongside people on the edges of the church and of society yet who is also secure and centred for themselves;*

- *an outgoing, risk-taking, world-oriented perspective;*

- *evidence of engagement with and in the local community, and awareness of what is happening in the wider world;*

- *evidence of a life of service within and outside the Christian community;*

- *evidence of ability to relate to people of different ages and social contexts;*

- *an instinctive ability to get alongside people and speak their language;*

- *pastoral skills that point to an ability to care for others appropriately;*

- *communication skills that enable the person to preach the gospel in deed and in word;*

- *teaching gifts, expressed in various and appropriate ways;*

- *liturgical sensitivity and presence that enables others to worship, brings the needs of the world into worship and interprets them for the Christian community;*

- *a rooted Christian spirituality, grounded in a life of prayer and immersion in God's word, attentive to God's presence in the world in its majesty and its misery;*

in caring for the poor, the needy, the sick, and all who are in trouble. He is to strengthen the faithful, search out the careless and indifferent, and to preach the word of God in the place to which he is licensed. A deacon assists the priest under whom he serves, in leading the worship of the people, especially in the administration of the Holy Communion. He may baptise when required to do so. It is his general duty to do such pastoral work as is entrusted to him.

Here there is a sense of the deacon being fully involved in, and not standing apart from the life and mission of the people of God. A threefold ministry of word, sacrament and pastoral care is envisaged for the deacon. It is clear that, although the deacon has a distinctive ministry, he (or she) does not have the cure of souls but assists those who do. However, the statement does not reflect the recently discovered insight that in Scripture *diakonia* is the service of God's Church because it is primarily the service of God. Moreover, while the relationship to the parish priest is emphasised, regrettably it is not expressed in a collegial way. It would have been better to have shown that the deacon has a distinctive ministry, alongside the parish priest, albeit under his or her oversight. The deacon's relationship to the bishop is not explicit here, though it is of course implied by the fact that it is the bishop (and the bishop alone in the case of deacons) who is ordaining.

The two movements of the Church's mission - sending and gathering - are suggested by the references to caring for those in need and searching out those who have drifted away, on the one hand, and leading worship and strengthening the faithful, on the other. But, regrettably, there is no mention of the deacon's involvement in social issues of justice, community-building, etc., and of bringing these to the heart of the Church's life through the liturgy.

So, although this statement could benefit from some fine tuning and the making explicit of what is implicit, there are actually sufficient theological resources in the current ordinal to support the thrust of the present report. In this report, we are advocating an approach that is already recognised - and to some extent practised.

The evidence from Scripture, history, ecumenical theology and the experience of our partner churches leads us to see the diaconate as a fundamental expression of apostolic ministry. Deacons are sent and commissioned by God. They serve the risen Christ, who is Lord and Head of the Church. Because they serve the Lord, they serve his people, both their fellow Christians and all God's children in their several needs. They are agents of the ministry of Christ himself.

The special role of deacons is to make connections and build bridges between the distinctive life, the *koinonia*, of the Body of Christ and the needs of the world. They can help build up the visibility of the Church by forging relationships, as ordained representative ministers, with the local community and - on a diocesan and regional basis - with civil society. For example, deacons can help to link the Church's mission with initiatives in urban regeneration or tackling rural deprivation.

Their go-between character also brings deacons into close association with the bishop and with the bishop's colleagues, the presbyters of the diocese. It also brings them into intimate contact with committed lay people and sets them alongside recognised lay ministries. The calling of deacons is to focus, to encourage and to help coordinate the *diakonia* (the divine commission) of the whole Church within the mission of God in the world and to do this in three ways: through the liturgy, through pastoral outreach and through catechetical work. The huge challenges that face the Church's mission today lead us to ask whether we have taken the diaconate as seriously as we should have done and to question more than ever its current mainly transitional function. Deacons can help the Church to connect. They are a major missing link in the Church's ministry and mission.

Like many other clergy, deacons today are involved in a wide range of creative and innovative activities, bringing the values of the gospel to the worlds of the arts, education, therapy, community development, and many more. While we honour all these forms of Christian service, we do not cite them all as models of diaconal ministry. We try to focus on what is specific to deacons, what they are ordained for, not on what they might become involved with as Christian individuals alongside lay people and other clergy. We identify the distinctive ministry of deacons by reference to the three criteria of the ministry of the word, the sacrament and pastoral care, where all three are exercised in a representative way under episcopal and presbyteral oversight.

It is worth underlining here that deacons should certainly take part in the conciliar life of the Church at every level and may stand for election to various synods. They should play a full part in deanery chapters and local clergy fraternals. Their ministry may particularly lend itself to ecumenical collaboration. In all these spheres, it is important that the distinctive voice of the diaconate should be heard.

The ministerial profile of the deacon will, then, include pastoral, liturgical and catechetical elements. These are not discrete elements in the life of the Church but are interrelated. They form the cycle of mission, a cycle that individuals may enter at any of the three points. All three are incorporated here in a missiological sense.

Pastoral

Pastoral care includes not simply the loving support of faithful members of the local Christian community, but also pastoral outreach to those (as the ASB Ordinal suggests) who have backslidden from church attendance or whose faith has become weak and troubled. By some accounts, more than half the population of England has drifted from earlier contact with the Christian Church. Such outreach must also, of course, include those who have had little past contact with the Church and for whom a link needs to be forged for the first time. The total constituency of the unchurched comprises a vast mission field where deacons, working with lay people who can devote themselves to this work, are needed. In the present state of our society, where there is a hunger for spiritual meaning combined with an indifference towards the institutional face of the churches, pastoral outreach is at the cutting edge of mission and should be seen as a form of evangelism. Church Army Evangelists model a compassionate form of pastoral outreach in the cause of mission. Deacons also may be encouraged to specialise in evangelism. This role is certainly consistent with the understanding of the deacon as an out-reaching minister of the gospel. But a rounded view of evangelism will not detach it from the pastoral mission of the Church or from the ministry of the word and sacraments, to both of which deacons are ordained. The bridging, go-between aspect of the deacon's ministry becomes particularly significant at this point.

The Church builds trust and respect in the community for its message when it gets alongside individuals, households and local organisations and institutions in a personal way. General pastoral visitation of the parish is perhaps now one of the weakest aspects of the Church's ministry, for various reasons. But the fact is that people respond best of all to a personal approach. Words alone cut little ice. Loving concern and practical support are the best ambassadors of the gospel in a largely post-Christian culture.

In this context, the vital pastoral role that deacons can play will vary according to their individual gifts and the needs of the parish. In teams of ordained and lay ministers, deacons may specialise in one or more particular areas of pastoral ministry, such as:

- Having a special care for the poor, the sick, the lonely and those who are ground down by adverse circumstances or by the pressures of life at home or work.

- Breaking new ground, as go-between persons, reaching parts of the community that are largely untouched by the regular ministry of the Church ('a safe foothold to a place beyond'); representing the Church and its Lord at the margins of society and beyond the normal boundaries of the Church, 'reaching into the forgotten corners of the world' (for example, making contact with hostels for the homeless and with families in bed and breakfast accommodation).

- Being an authorised prophetic voice on behalf of justice and working for change in oppressive and unjust structures.

- Helping to set up new networks and to gather fresh resources for pastoral outreach, so helping to draw individuals and families into the community of the Church.

- Modelling and encouraging outreach to help motivate some less confident lay people to witness to their faith by entering into collaboration with them.

- Towards a ministerial profile

- Leading and coordinating general pastoral visiting in the parish, keeping track of new arrivals in the neighbourhood and of special pastoral needs and providing continuity and coherence.

- Having a special concern for young families, especially among the unchurched; working to bring them within the ambit of the Church's means of grace through pram services, crib services, parent and toddler groups, etc.

- Developing a special ministry in schools and youth organisations, hospitals and prisons.

- Being the focal ministry person, in collaboration with the parish priest, in a particular area within the benefice where the deacon, but not the priest happens to live.

Liturgical

Deacons embody the *sine qua non* of the Church's mission: that it should be grounded in and never lose touch with the liturgical life of the Church, made up of word and sacrament, praise and intercession. Deacons have a distinctive ministry in the celebration of the liturgy, assisting the bishop or priest who is presiding. In particular, in their go-between role, they bring into worship the concerns and hopes of all God's children that these may be lifted up to the throne of grace.

The deacon's liturgical ministry is recognised in the rubrics of *Common Worship* and may include:

- Ministering at the celebration of the Eucharist in ways that are appropriate to the life of the community and without excluding the ministry of lay people: reading the Gospel, leading the prayers of penitence, the intercessions and the acclamations of the people, inviting the exchange of the peace, serving at the altar, administering Holy Communion, and sending out the people with the liturgical dismissal.

- Conducting the daily offices and other non-eucharistic liturgical services, especially Morning and Evening Prayer.

- Officiating at baptism at the request of the parish priest.

- Ordering the church or cathedral liturgically for the community's worship, with special regard to preparing the font and the altar, supporting and guiding the sacristan or verger.

- Conducting house and hospital communions with the sacrament reserved for the sick and housebound and officiating at services of the word with the administration of Holy Communion ('extended communion').

- Assisting and (except in their first year) officiating at marriages.

- Conducting funeral services and burials.

- Ministering to the sick and the dying with prayers.

Catechetical

Deacons in the Church of England are ordained also to the ministry of the word of God. They are called and trained to preach and to teach. They carry out this ministry in collaboration with and under the oversight of the parish priest and both deacon and priest are subject to the oversight of the bishop who is called to be a guardian of sound doctrine. This aspect of the deacon's ministry overlaps with those of Reader, presbyter and bishop. Once again, there is scope for specialisation according to need and gift, including:

- Coordinating and monitoring faith-development courses, such as Alpha and Emmaus, and Lent courses (including working with other churches where these courses are run ecumenically) and working with the parish priest to follow up the opportunities these provide.

- Preparing candidates (or their parents) for baptism.

- Preaching in the liturgy.

- Conducting Confirmation preparation.

- Preparing couples for marriage.

- Where some of these catechetical tasks are carried out by trained lay people, to help train the trainers, to support and guide them in this work

- Supporting and guiding lay people's involvement in such children's activities as After School and Holiday Clubs.

- Specialist counselling, seen as being on behalf of the Church, to those diagnosed with HIV/AIDS or those addicted to various forms of substance abuse.

- Training volunteers to befriend families in need.

- Representing the Church's concerns and priorities, on behalf of the bishop, in areas of community action and in relation to major institutions within the diocese (local and regional government, urban regeneration initiatives, the health service, the world of education, the voluntary sector, etc.). Such specific areas of mission should be decided in discussion with the bishop before ordination and licensing.

- Training and teaching roles within the diocese, archdeaconry or deanery. (It would seem appropriate for a person carrying out this form of the ministry of the word, with the bishop's commission, and who was not called to oversight and to presidency at the Eucharist, to remain a deacon.)

Clarifying the role of deacon

In relation to ordained ministry, it is important that the advent of a renewed diaconate should help to clarify the differentiation of the threefold ministry and other authorized ministries. It is widely recognized that a one-year transitional diaconate does not enhance clarity about this ministry. Questions are frequently raised as to whether the reality of the deacon's ministry can be authentically experienced in this brief period. Although overlap is endemic in all forms of ministry, a renewed diaconate should not add to existing grey areas and blurred edges but should assist clarity.

In relation to lay ministry, a renewed diaconate should on no account absorb expressions of ministry that are entrusted to lay people. In parishes where lay ministry already flourishes, deacons will help to support, guide and coordinate this. It is not for them to seek to control it or to try to take it over. They will be well advised to be supportive in the background until their enabling and training gifts are invited. In parishes where lay ministry has barely got off the ground, deacons will focus, model and pioneer expressions of ministry to which lay people may be called, helping to release talents and energy within the community and then taking a back seat as much as possible.

Although deacons must be rooted in the liturgical life of the Church, especially the Eucharist, the main focus of the work that they do will be in the wider world where they represent the Church as an ordered community under the leadership of bishops and priests. Their liturgical role can helpfully be seen as an oblation of this ministry to God. They should not become simply liturgical functionaries. Mission remains the litmus test of ministry and a deacon is primarily a missionary.

Deacons in administration?

It is sometimes suggested that deacons might specialise in church administration, perhaps in support of the bishop. The roles of bishop's chaplain and of archdeacon are sometimes cited. Of course, it is not the administrative duties alone of either a bishop's chaplain or an archdeacon that make it appropriate for that person to be ordained. One does not need to be ordained to do office work or other administrative chores or to liaise with the bishop's co-workers or to organise meetings or to draft letters for the bishop.

It is primarily the liturgical role of the bishop's chaplain – combined perhaps with a pastoral role to individuals on behalf of the bishop – that makes ordination appropriate. If the chaplain is not to have pastoral charge of a parish and is not required to preside at the Eucharist, then it makes sense for him or her to be a deacon.

It might well be appropriate for a person who leads and coordinates a charitable agency of the Church to be a deacon, provided it can be seen in each case that it is a role that belongs properly to the ordained. A commissioning to direct work that is primarily pastoral in nature, provided that it included some elements of the ministry of the word and/or the sacraments, would seem to fit this criterion.

Archdeacons in deacons' orders have been a tradition in Orthodoxy and have been reinvented recently in the Episcopal Church of the USA and in the Diocese of Brisbane. However, this practice seems questionable to us. Even if an archdeacon is never going to preside at the Eucharist, which would seem an undue restriction of that ministry, he or she certainly exercises oversight, sometimes in the form of discipline, on behalf of the diocesan bishop. Presbyters directly share the bishop's oversight; deacons do not. The Church of England's Canons (C 22) emphasise the jurisdiction of the archdeacon as ordinary and that would seem to be the basis of the canonical requirement that archdeacons shall be in priest's orders.

Deacons in pastoral charge?

For similar reasons, we would not expect a deacon to be placed in pastoral charge of a parish, even temporarily. Deacons are not ordained to oversight but to a ministry of assistance to and collaboration with those in oversight. This restriction, that is inherent in the nature of their order, should not be taken as preventing deacons from showing leadership in specific areas of Church work or from being put forward by the incumbent as the focal pastoral person in a particular community within, say, a multi-parish benefice. A degree of prominence is entailed in any representative ministry, whether lay or ordained, but this is a different matter from having formal pastoral charge, the cure of souls and being accountable to the bishop for that. When deacons are put in positions of oversight, serious distortion of their calling ensues. We are clear that pastoral charge is one area that is definitely not right for the deacon.

Deacons as ministers in secular employment

We are not assuming in this report that distinctive deacons will necessarily be non-stipendiary. But obviously some, perhaps a considerable proportion, will be self-financing. So there will be deacons who will exercise their diaconal ministry in church and in the parish community but will have a so-called secular job as well. Some may have the opportunity to exercise a diaconal ministry (one that is liturgical, pastoral and catechetical) in their place of work with the permission of their employer and the goodwill of their colleagues. But this is a sensitive area and demands wisdom, restraint and patience until the Lord opens the door that no one can shut (cf. Revelation 3.8)

Looking at the matter another way, what about ordaining deacon a person who has a noted ministry, as a lay person, in their place of work? Once again, we must not appear to detract from the integrity of lay ministry and witness. We would not expect a Minister in Secular Employment to be ordained either deacon or priest unless there was a specific representative ministry of word, sacrament and pastoral care that could be discerned in that person's work situation. All Christians serve the Lord in their daily calling, whether at home, in the local community, or in another place of work. They witness to their faith in various informal ways. We would be looking for a special representative role, normally recognized in some way by the person's employer and work colleagues, before we would consider ordination appropriate.

Having said that, if a representative ministry of leading worship, teaching the faith and extending pastoral care should develop, it would seem right for the individual concerned to have his or her vocation to the diaconate tested. Given that recognized role in certain cases, we would judge ordination to the diaconate, rather than to the priesthood, to be appropriate for a person who would not be sharing directly in pastoral oversight and would not be presiding at the Eucharist.

1   Church of England Working Party of the House of Bishops (2001) *For such a time as this*' London: Church House Publishing

2   Correspondence from The Revd. Dr. Roly Riem

3   Mrs Viviane Hall, in the General Synod debate on 'For such a time as this'.

4   In particular, 'The Diocese of Salisbury Ordained Local Ministry Scheme'. Revised Edition. December 1999, Bishop David Stancliffe's papers, 'Celebrating Ordination: Towards the reshaping of the ASB Ordinal for Common Worship' and 'The Diaconate: A Paper for the IALC' (August 1999) and The Revd. Dr Ian Paul's paper, 'Reflections on the Diocesan Theology of Ministry' (July 2001).

5   Derived primarily from the OLM submission

6   Derived from 'Celebrating Ordination' and 'The Diaconate', quoting in part from the World Council of Churches Faith and Order Commission.

7   'Baptism, Eucharist and Ministry'. (1982). WCC

8   Derived from 'For such a time as this' chapter 3.

9   Collins, J (1990) 'Diakonia: Reinterpreting the Ancient Sources' Oxford: OUP

10   Derived from 'for such a time as this' Chapter 5.

11   Borgegard, G, Fanuelsen, O, Hall, C, (1999) 'The Ministry of the Deacon' Volume 1: Anglican-Lutheran Perspectives' and Borgegard, G and, Hall, C, (2000) 'The Ministry of the Deacon' Volume 2: Ecclesiological Explorations. Uppsala: Nordic Ecumenical Council

12   Kuhrt, G and Nappin, P (eds) (2002) 'Bridging the Gap' London: Church House Publishing

13   Headley, Carolyn, (2000) 'Readers and Worship in the Church of England'. Cambridge: Grove Books

14   Mr Nigel Chetwood, in the General Synod debate on 'For such a time as this'.

15   Hall, Christine 'The Deacon in the Church of England' in Borgegard, Faunelson and Hall (1999)

16   Brodd, Sven-Eric, '*Caritas and Diakonia* as Perspectives on the Diaconate' in Borgegard and Hall (2000)

17   Monroe Barnett, J (1979, 1995) 'The Diaconate: a Full and Equal Order', Harrisburg: Trinity Press International. Pages 19-42

18   Collins, John N (2002) *Deacons and the Church* Leominster: Gracewing

19   Collins (2002) pp 47-58

20   Good, Deidre (1999)' Jesus the Meek King'. Harrisburg: Trinity Press International

21   Wijngaards, John (2002) 'No Women in Holy Orders?' Norwich: Canterbury Press. Pages 10,12

22   Fiddes, Paul (2000) 'Participating in God'. London: DLT (p71-72)

23   Croft, Stephen (1999) 'Ministry in Three Dimensions' London: DLT

24   Barnett (1979,1995) p54

25   The Apostolic Tradition of Hippolytus 9:2-4

26   The Epistle of Clement to James 8:220

27 Antonia Lynn 'Finding Images' in Hall, C (ed) 1991, 'The Deacon's Ministry' Leominster: Gracewing. Page 104.

28 Hall, C, in Borgegard, Fanuelson and Hall (2000). Page 103.

29 Yanneras, C (1991) 'Elements of Faith: an Introduction to Orthodox Theology'. Edinburgh. Page 139.

30 Brodd, S-E in Borgegard, Fanuelson and Hall (2000). Page 36

31 Brodd, S-E in Borgegard, Fanuelson and Hall (2000). Page 64

32 Schillebeeckx, Edward (1985) 'The Church with a Human Face' London: SCM. Page 39. We are grateful to Roly Riem for pointing out the ideas in this paragraph.

33 The Fourth World Conference of Faith and Order. Montreal 1963.

34 Summarised in 'For such a time as this' chapter 3.

35 See section 2.7

36 'For such a time as this' chapter 2.

37 'Deacons in the Ministry of the Church' A Report to the House of Bishops, 1988

38 Lambeth Conference 1958, Recommendation 88

39 Lambeth Conference 1988, 'Reviewing the Diaconate.' Paragraph 121

40 Lambeth Conference 1998, 'Called to be faithful in a plural world.' Paragraphs 88, 90.

41 Lambeth Conference 1998, 'Called to be faithful in a plural world.' Paragraph 91

42 'For such a time as this'. Chapter 3

43 Dogmatic Constitution on the Church. Lumen Gentium 41

44 'De Ecclesia, The Constitution of the Church of Vatican II Proclaimed by Pope Paul VI, 21st November 1964. Paragraph 29, and 'Approval of a New Rite for the Ordination of Deacons, Priests and Bishops' Apostolic Constitution 18th June 1968.

45 Dogmatic Constitution on the Church. Lumen Gentium 41

46 'The Permanent Diaconate'. Catholic Truth Society 1988.

47 Answer given at the Second National Diaconal Assembly. 1998.

48 'For such a time as this.' Chapter 3

49 Melan, Roar, 'The Deacon in the Church of Norway' in Borgegard, Fanelson and Hall (1999)

50 Brodd, Sven-Erik, 'The Deacon in the Church of Sweden' in Borgegard, Fanuelson and Hall (1999)

51 Pohjolainen, Terttu, 'The Deacon in the Evangelical-Lutheran Church of Finland' in Borgegard, Fanuelson and Hall (1999)

52 The United Reformed Church web site

53 Jackson, Sue 'What is a Deacon' in Luscombe, P and Shreeve, E (2002) 'What is a Minister' Peterborough: Epworth Press

54 Howcroft, Kenneth 'Ministerial Roles in Methodism' in Luscombe and Shreeve op.cit.

55   The United Methodist Church web site, 'The Ministry of the Deacon.'

56   Aitchison, Ronnie (2003) 'The Ministry of a Deacon' Peterborough: Epworth Press

57   Aitchison, R (2003) *op. cit.*. Pages 161,153, 162, 152

58   Ecumenical Patriarchate Inter-Orthodox Theological Consultation, Rhodes 1988.VIII. 32,34

59   The Porvoo Common Statement (1993) Paragraph 32j

60   The Porvoo Common Statement (1993) Paragraph 58b (vii)

61   Norgren, W. 'A Commentary on Called to Common Mission' ECUSA web site.

62   The Fetter Lane Agreement website.

63   'For such a time as this.' Chapter 3

64   'Commitment to Mission and Unity: A Report of Informal Consultations between the Church of England and the Methodist Church', 1996. Para 20

65   The Anglican / Methodist International Commission. 'Sharing in the Apostolic Communion' 1996, 50,51,53

66   The Anglican-Lutheran International Commission. 'The Hanover Report', 1996. Para 79

67   'The Windsor Statement on the Diaconate' (1997), issued following a consultation between the Church of Scotland, the Scottish Episcopal Church, the British Methodist Church, the Roman Catholic Church and the Church of England. The consultation included conversations with a United Reformed Church CRCW and a Deacon in training in the Orthodox Church.

68   Trial liturgy for the Ordination of Deacons in use in the Diocese of Salisbury, 2002.

69   The Alternative Service Book: Ordination of Deacons.

70   Common Worship: Service and Prayers for the Church of England. (2000) Page 158.

71   Perham, Michael (2000) New Handbook of Pastoral Liturgy. London: SPCK. Page 34.

72   Kavanagh, Aidan (1990) Elements of Rite: A Handbook of Liturgical Style. Pueblo.

73   'For such a time as this' Page 54

74   Based, in part, on 'For such a time as this.' Chapter 7.

75   Aitchison, R *op cit* Page 152

76   (General Synod (1987) The Liturgical Ministry of Deacons: A Report by the Liturgical Commission. London: Church House Publishing. Paragraphs 18–22.

77   Seifert, R. J. (1995) 'Hermes as Proto-Deacon: an Examination of Preaching and the Diaconate. Washington: College of Preachers

78   Hooker, R. 'Laws of Ecclesiastical Polity' V.18

79   Hall, C in Borgegard, Fanuelson and Hall (1999). Page 203

80   Hall, C in Borgegard, Fanuelson and Hall (1999). Pages 203–210

81   Information from the Diocesan Director of Ordinands (NSM)

82 This comment is based on a misapprehension of the current OLM selection process.

83 'For such a time as this.' Chapter 8.

84 'For such a time as this.' Chapter 6.

85 The Methodist Church. (2001) 'Information Sheet for Training Institutions regarding Diaconal Students'

86 Smedberg, Ninni 'The Quest for a Spirituality for the Deacon' in Borgegard, Fanuelsen and Hall (2000)

87 Fitzgerald, K.K. (1999) 'Women Deacons in the Orthodox Church, Called to Holiness and Ministry' quoted in Smedberg, N *op cit* Page 147.

88 Kasper, W (1997) 'The Deacon offers an ecclesiological view of the present day challenges in the Church and Society' Paper at IDC Study Conference. Brixen, Italy